Italy in the Twentieth Century

CHARLES F. DELZELL

WITHDRAWN

AMERICAN HISTORICAL ASSOCIATION
AHA PAMPHLETS
428

Italy in the Twentieth Century

CHARLES F. DELZELL

428 AHA PAMPHLETS
AMERICAN HISTORICAL ASSOCIATION
400 A Street, SE, Washington, D.C. 20003

CHARLES F. DELZELL is professor of history at Vanderbilt University, where he has been since 1952. Previously he taught at the University of Hawaii, University of Oregon, and was Curator of Mediterranean Collections in the Hoover Institution at Stanford University. He received the BS from the University of Oregon, the AM and PhD from Stanford University, and studied at the Istituto Italiano per gli Studi Storici in Naples. His research interests are modern Italian and European history. He is the author of *Mussolini's Enemies: The Italian Anti-Fascist Resistance* (1961; reprint, 1974) and *Italy in Modern Times* (1964). With John L. Snell he coauthored *The Meaning of Yalta* (1956) and, with Hans Schmitt, *Historians of Modern Europe* (1971). He is a frequent contributor to the *Encyclopedia Americana* and has edited *The Unification of Italy, 1859-1861* (1965); *Mediterranean Fascism, 1919-1945* (1970); *The Papacy and Totalitarianism Between the Two World Wars* (1974); and *The Future of History* (1977). He has held Fulbright and NEH Senior fellowships and a residency at the Rockefeller Study and Conference Center in Bellagio, Italy. He has been President of the Society for Italian Historical Studies, the American Committee on the History of the Second World War, the European Section of the Southern Historical Association, and a member of the Council of the AHA.

© Copyright, THE AMERICAN HISTORICAL ASSOCIATION,
1980

All rights reserved. No part of this book may be reproduced in any form without permission in writing from the publisher, except by a reviewer who wishes to quote brief passages in connection with the review written for inclusion in a magazine or newspaper. The American Historical Association does not adopt official views on any field of history and does not necessarily agree or disagree with the views expressed in this book.

ISBN 0-87229-024-7
Library of Congress Catalog Card Number: 80-71044
Composed and printed at

Printed in the United States of America

Italy in the Twentieth Century

CHARLES F. DELZELL

In the nineteenth century Italy was among the last major European countries to achieve national unification. Its liberal parliamentary system was approaching democratic maturity when World War I interrupted its evolution. In the twentieth century Italy was the first European country to discard such a system in favor of a Fascist government (1922). Headed by Benito Mussolini, this government transformed itself within a few years into a totalitarian dictatorship. Mussolini had founded his movement in 1919 amidst the socioeconomic and political dislocations brought about by Italy's participation in the Great War and in the face of widespread, though probably exaggerated, fears of bolshevism coming to power. After some initial wavering, the Blackshirt Fascist movement quickly found a niche in Italy's political spectrum as a new "radicalism of the Right."

Despite its readiness to use force, Mussolini's ultranationalistic and militaristic regime succeeded in mobilizing and indoctrinating the masses, thereby achieving considerable popularity both at home and abroad during the 1920s and early 1930s. It repudiated Marxist "dialectical materialism" and called instead for class conciliation and idealism. Although much of the so-called Corporative State that the Duce of Fascism erected turned out to be a tumbling house of cards in 1943, his Lateran pacts with the Vatican in February 1929 proved more enduring. After Mussolini decided to form an Axis alliance with Adolf Hitler and undertook a series of wars that eventually led to repeated disasters, however, the great majority of

Italians lost confidence in their Duce. On July 25, 1943, the Fascist regime was overthrown in a coup d'état carried out by King Victor Emmanuel III, Marshal Pietro Badoglio, and others. A few weeks later they surrendered to the invading armies of the Anglo-Americans, who propped them up in the liberated southern portion of the peninsula. Simultaneously, Hitler's forces quickly seized control of Rome and northern Italy, where they reinstated the ailing Mussolini to nominal authority in a new "Italian Social Republic" for two more years.

A powerful underground Armed Resistance movement in the North helped the Allies greatly in bringing about the final liberation of all the country by April 25, 1945. Resistance leaders captured the fleeing Mussolini and executed him. But Fascism and its Duce were not the only casualties of the war. In a referendum held on June 2, 1946, the electorate, which now included women, voted narrowly to discard the monarchy, chiefly because of its twenty years of close association with Fascism. The deep-seated cultural, socioeconomic, and political differences between Italy's North and South were revealed once again in that referendum. Rome and the North voted solidly republican, whereas the South remained royalist; but many of the other dreams of left-wing Resistance leaders for a thorough renovation of Italy remained unfulfilled. Thus there occurred, at least in the judgment of many on the Left, yet another *rivoluzione mancata* ("failed revolution"), so common in Italian history. Nevertheless, a new republican constitution was drawn up by the Constituent Assembly in 1947. Its most striking innovation was provision for twenty regional governments—a program that was not fully implemented until 1970.

Italy, which under Fascism had been ultranationalistic, now quickly joined the ranks of the free world. In 1949, during the Cold War, it became a charter member of the North Atlantic Treaty Organization, but the stalemate between East and West delayed Italy's admission to the United Nations until 1955. A couple of years later, upon the signing of the Treaties of Rome, Italy became a cofounder of the European Economic Community. Indeed, Italy is one of the most European-minded members of the various communities. Her own constitution is unique in making possible the surrender of considerable national sovereignty to such supranational bodies.

Beginning in the 1950s Italy experienced an "economic miracle"—a vast program of industrialization, road building, and socioeconomic change that has greatly transformed and modernized the country, putting it among the top ten industrial states in the world. The new industries in the North have attracted a spontaneous outmigration of millions of peasants from the South, many of whom have continued on across the Alps to become "guest workers" in Germany and elsewhere. There has also been important economic growth in the South, but the disparity between the two regions remains substantial and in some respects has increased. Italy has also experienced a cultural renaissance since the overthrow of the stultifying Fascist dictatorship. Thus, Italians once again have revealed their genius, especially in the fields of literature, cinematography, architecture, and art.

But there are darker sides to the Italian scene. The postwar political class and the enormous bureaucracy have not functioned well. The Christian Democratic party—heavily faction-ridden and only partially attuned to the rapidly changing modern world—has managed to head every government since December 1945, sometimes only with the shaky help of one or more of the small centrist parties. The Communists are the major opposition party and continue to enjoy the support of one out of every four voters. Since 1956 this party has insisted upon a "polycentrist" policy of autonomy from Moscow and, more recently under the leadership of Enrico Berlinguer, has advocated "Eurocommunism." The Italian Socialist party has experienced numerous splits since the war but has now regrouped, discarded its old Marxist rhetoric, and augmented its appeal to middle-class voters. Italy's Christian Democratic governments remain highly vulnerable; indeed, they survive only at the sufferance of either the Socialists or the Communists.

Terrorism is another chronic problem. The present underground terrorist groups emerged in the aftermath of the university upheavals of 1968/69 and operate on both the extreme Left and extreme Right. Thus far, however, the structure of the Italian state has held firm in the face of their onslaughts.

Finally, among the major problems confronting Italy are the energy crisis and inflation, both of which have been greatly aggravated by OPEC's drastic increases in the price of oil since 1973. The resulting malaise has caused Italy to share with Britain the dubious distinction of being the "sick men" of the European Economic Community—though in Italy's case there is no North Sea oil to help remedy the problem. There is some reason, however, for hope. To be sure, Italians are cynical and skeptical, but over their long history they have repeatedly displayed a knack for "muddling through" and surmounting their difficulties through a combination of hard work, patience, and ingenuity.

The kaleidoscopic events sketched briefly above have inspired a large body of scholarly and journalistic literature that attempts to explain them. The historiographical essay that follows will focus primarily on studies in English, particularly on those that have appeared during the past twenty years and which show familiarity with current Italian scholarship. But passing attention will also be given to major studies in Italian and other languages. First of all, however, a few observations should be made regarding the current trends and problems in writing Italian history of the twentieth century.

Bibliographical Essay

It has taken much longer to develop a corpus of historical scholarship on Fascist Italy than on Nazi Germany. This was partly because only a relatively small amount of Fascist records fell into Allied hands in 1943–45, in contrast to the situation in Germany at the end of the war. Even so, it was to be Anglo-American specialists who did most of the writing in the early postwar period on Italy's Fascist dictatorship.[1] Most of Italy's own scholars—apart from dedicated anti-Fascist historians like Gaetano Salvemini, Luigi Salvatorelli, Giovanni Mira, Nino Valeri, Federico Chabod, and Aldo Garosci, as well as certain others who were in a mood to write memorialist literature[2]—seemed to prefer to devote their attention to less controversial eras. Often this was because they did not yet have access to the appropriate archival material; in other instances, it was perhaps the result of reluctance to write about a regime with which

---

[1]Fifty years of American scholarship on Fascist Italy are reviewed by Philip V. Cannistraro in "Il fascismo italiano visto dagli Stati Uniti: Cinquant'anni di studi e di interpretazioni," *Storia contemporanea* 2 (Sept. 1971): 599–622. See also Charles F. Delzell, "Studi americani sul fascismo," *Il Nuovo Osservatore: Politico-economico-sociale* (Rome), 56/57 (Nov.–Dec. 1966), pp. 952–62.

[2]On literature of this sort, see Emiliana P. Noether, "Italy Reviews her Fascist Past," *American Historical Review* 61 (July 1956): 877–99. I wish to take this opportunity to express my gratitude to Professor Noether for some helpful suggestions while I was preparing this pamphlet. She is not to blame for any inaccuracies, however.

many of them had experienced too recent a relationship. In any case, it was chiefly historians who emerged from the victorious anti-Fascist Resistance who were ready to write on this period, and there was an initial tendency, of course, for them to be one-sided in expressing judgments on Fascism.

This attitude of benign neglect was to be altered by three major events that shook up Italian historiography. In 1955 the Tenth International Congress of the Historical Sciences met in Rome, thereby enabling Italian students to become better acquainted with new foreign trends in historiography, including that of the *Annales* school of social history in France. Moreover, Nikita Khrushchev's denunciation of Stalin in February 1956 and the ensuing Hungarian revolution which was brutally suppressed by the Russians that autumn caused disillusionment among many Italian Marxist intellectuals with the Kremlin versions of history. More objective scholarship regarding the history of the Italian Communist Party and of the Third International was now undertaken, as well as of other topics. Even more important was the veritable explosion of rebelliousness on the part of a burgeoning cohort of postwar students in 1968 who were seeking "relevance" in Italy's overcrowded universities—a phenomenon that had its counterpart in many other countries and which was aggravated by the controversies stirred by the American intervention in the Vietnam war. This led to major restructuring of the Italian universities and curricula and induced many young scholars to reexamine their country's contemporary history. They often undertook this assignment in a frankly partisan spirit. Indeed, probably nowhere else in Western Europe do considerations of political ideology influence historical research as much as they do in Italy.

Thus, three major historiographical currents have dominated the field since the war. The older liberal-democratic school is challenged increasingly by Marxist (Italian style) and Catholic currents. The Marxists claim to have the winds of history blowing in their favor. The Catholic writers share with the Communists a hostility to the liberal-democratic tradition but they seem to lack an autonomous Catholic political culture of their own. Despite the partisanship that is displayed in almost all sectors, giant strides have been made in reassessing the Fascist era and other aspects of Italy's recent history.

A host of problems confront the new discipline of contemporary history in Italy. First of all, there are far too few professors trained in this field. Until recently there has been relatively little "social-scientization" of history, i.e., the integration of the new quantitative methodologies developed by the other social sciences. Since about 1977, however, there has been a noticeable shift toward the new methodologies espoused by the *Annales* school in France. Intellectual history continues to be elitist and closer to philosophy than to sociology. Italians evince little or no interest in psychohistory, family history, or women's history. Nor has much been done in the field of oral history. Access to the holdings in Rome's Archivio Centrale dello Stato is governed by the 50-year rule, although some exceptions have been made for established scholars working on topics pertaining to the pre-1943 period. Consultation of the Archivio Storico del Ministero degli Affari Esteri and those of the armed services is even more tightly restricted.[3] Italian historians tend to remain parochial in their interests; seldom do they branch out to consider the histories of other countries or the problems of comparative history. Nor are they much inclined to move beyond narrow monographs to the writing of history that covers an extended period of time.[4]

Wide-ranging and often incisive discussions in English of recent historiographical trends in Italy may be found in the following articles: Alan Cassels, "Italian Fascism Comes of Age: The Problem of an Adequate Historiography," *Cesare Barbieri Courier: A Special Issue on Mussolini and Italian Fascism,* Trinity College (Hartford, Conn., 1980), pp. 14-24; Renzo De Felice, "Italian Historiography since the Second World War," *Altro Polo, A Volume of Italian Studies,* ed. Richard J. B. Bosworth and Gianfranco Cresciani (Sydney, Australia, 1979), pp. 161-82; A. William Salomone, "Italy," *International Handbook of Historical Studies: Contemporary Research and Theory,* ed. Georg G. Iggers and Harold T. Parker (Westport, Conn., 1979), pp. 233-51; Marino Berengo, "Italian Historical Scholarship since the Fascist Era," *Daedalus* (Spring 1971): 469-84; Claudio

---

[3]See the section on Italy by Vincent Ilardi and Mary L. Shay in *The New Guide to the Diplomatic Archives of Western Europe,* ed. D. H. Thomas and Lynn M. Case (Philadelphia, 1975), and the Council for European Studies pamphlet, *Guide to Italian Libraries and Archives,* ed. R. J. and R. C. Lewanski (New York, 1979).

[4]See the comments on these points by Alberto Aquarone, Paolo Ungari, and Stefano Rodotà, eds., *Gli studi di storia e di diritto contemporaneo* (Milan, 1968), pp. 15-92, which also includes a listing of postwar Italian studies on that country's contemporary history.

Pavone, "Italy: Trends and Problems," *Journal of Contemporary History* 2 (1967): 48-76; and Charles F. Delzell, "Italian Historical Scholarship: A Decade of Recovery and Development, 1945-1955," *Journal of Modern History* 28 (Dec. 1956): 374-88.

Italian academicians have a tradition of writing summaries of historiographical controversies, interspersed with references and suggestions for possible new areas for research. The most recent of these handbooks is the three-volume *Storia d'Italia: Il mondo contemporaneo* (Florence, 1978), ed. Fabio Levi, Umberto Levra, and Nicola Tranfaglia. Writing from a distinctly leftist perspective, its contributors discuss more than eighty topics.

A state-financed research center in Rome, the Istituto per la storia moderna e contemporanea, publishes a comprehensive *Bibliografia storica nazionale* (Bari: Laterza), which lists current historical scholarship in Italy pertaining to all periods. It may also be noted that there are a number of nongovernmentally-financed research centers. By way of example, for socialism, the labor movement, and economic history there are the Istituto Antonio Gramsci in Rome, the Fondazione Luigi Einaudi in Turin, and the Istituto Giangiacomo Feltrinelli in Milan, while for Catholic social history there is the Istituto Luigi Sturzo in Rome.

Prior to the 1950s the principal historical journals of a nonregional character in Italy were the *Rivista storica italiana* (dealing with all fields), the *Nuova rivista storica* (specializing in socioeconomic history), and the *Rassegna storica del Risorgimento* (focusing on Italy's liberal-national movement of unification). All three often accorded at least some attention to twentieth-century Italy. Postwar Marxist journals like *Società* and *Movimento operaio* gave way in the more relaxed ideological climate after de-Stalinization in 1956 to such new ones as *Movimento operaio e socialista* and *Studi storici*. The *Rivista storica del socialismo* was the most flexible in its outlook—classist but nonparty. Liberal journals, oriented toward Benedetto Croce's ethicopolitical, neoidealist historicism, included *Critica storica* and *Clio* in the 1960s. In 1970 Renzo De Felice, who was trained in the Crocean school though not exclusively so, began publishing his journal, *Storia contemporanea*. Two years later the Marxist and anti-De Felice journal, *Rivista di storia contemporanea*, started publication. The historical review of the Istituto nazionale per la storia del movimento di liberazione, *Movimento di liberazione in Italia*, changed its name in 1974 to

Italia contemporanea, broadening its scope to include the entire twentieth century. Recently increasing interest in the *Annales* school of history is reflected in three new journals: *Quaderni storici; Storia urbana;* and *Società e storia*.[5] Finally, in 1979, the English-language *Journal of Italian History* began publication in Florence under Ennio Di Nolfo's editorship. It contains articles and considerable bibliographical information about current historical controversies, though its focus is not restricted to the present century. Outside of Italy the *Journal of Contemporary History* (London), the *Journal of Modern History* (Chicago), the *American Historical Review* (Bloomington, Ind.), and the newly launched *Risorgimento: European Review for Italian Modern History* (Brussels) often contain articles and reviews that are relevant to contemporary Italy. Both the "Recently Published Articles" section on Italy compiled by Emiliana P. Noether in the *American Historical Review* and the article listings for Italy in *Historical Abstracts* (Santa Barbara, Calif.) are very helpful to the researcher. The above list of journals is not meant to be exhaustive.

General Histories of Twentieth-Century Italy

The most provocative general survey in English is *Italy: A Modern History* (Ann Arbor, 1969), by Denis Mack Smith of All Souls College, a work that is written from a radical, democratic perspective and covers in readable fashion all aspects of the period since unification in 1860. The author is familiar with current Italian scholarship, writes with coruscating wit, and is scathing in his criticisms of Mussolini's dictatorship. A good many Italian historians, including the liberal Rosario Romeo, are distressed, however, at Mack Smith's predisposition to view Fascism as the key to understanding the whole of Italian reality and his consequent tendency to push back the antecedents of Fascism not just to the 1890–1919 years but considerably earlier.

More restricted in its time frame is an excellent, sober study by another Oxonian, Christopher Seton-Watson, *Italy from Liberalism to Fascism: 1870–1925* (London, 1967). An epilogue presents an overview of the Fascist era. Moderate in its tone and careful in its judgments, Seton-Watson's book lacks, however, the verve of Mack Smith's account. It is thoroughly reliable and well annotated.

---

[5]See Stuart J. Woolf, "The new historical journals," London *Times Literary Supplement*, May 2, 1980, p. 503.

Updated and enlarged in a recent third edition is H. Stuart Hughes's pithy and lucid book, *The United States and Italy* (Cambridge, Mass., 1979). The author outlines the regional, economic, and psychological factors that have affected Italy's development and also considers the traditional contacts between Italy and the United States, but he concentrates most of his attention on the Fascist and post-World War II era. Hughes has a keen eye not only for political and social trends but for cultural developments. A couple of new chapters have been added to the third, revised edition: the first of these explains the social stresses which have resulted from rapid change, while the second assesses the current role of the Communist party. This is perhaps the best concise study in English to help one gain a clear understanding of contemporary Italy.

Another overview that can be read with profit is Muriel Grindrod, *Italy* (New York, 1968), though it is now somewhat dated. She spent many years researching Italian politics and economics for the Royal Institute of International Affairs. Her volume contains chapters on postwar economic conditions, Church-State relations, and the special problems posed by Sicily and Sardinia.

Two other books deal with a much longer time but include brief discussions of the twentieth century. One is entitled *Italy* (Englewood Cliffs, N.J., 1965), by Massimo Salvadori, an articulate advocate of liberalism; the other, *A History of the Italian People* (New York, 1970), by an Italian Communist historian, Giuliano Procacci. Both authors exercise scholarly restraint in their judgments. A French historian, Maurice Vaussard, has written a survey that is objective and moderate in tone: *Histoire de l'Italie moderne, 1870–1970* (Paris, 1971).

Thematic in structure is a work edited by Edward R. Tannenbaum and Emiliana P. Noether, *Modern Italy: A Topical History since 1861* (New York, 1974). The outgrowth of a conference at Columbia University, it contains essays by a dozen specialists on politics and ideology; economics and social developments; intellectual, religious, and cultural trends; and foreign policy. Most of the chapters are satisfactory and several are of distinct merit—particularly Raymond Grew's discussion of Catholicism, and the papers presented by foreign guests: Mack Smith's piece on regionalism; Rosario Romeo's Crocean-oriented essay on the impact of German high culture on Italy before the Great War; and Alberto Aquarone's thoughtful concluding observations, "Problems of democracy and the quest for identity."

There are half a dozen recent multivolume histories in Italian that focus on the contemporary era. Non-Marxist in its orientation is "Storia dell'Italia contemporanea" (Naples: Edizioni Scientifiche Italiane, 1978), directed by Renzo De Felice. Its five volumes cover the period from the 1890s to 1956. An older set, edited by Nino Valeri, "Storia d'Italia" (Turin: UTET, 1965), devotes its fifth volume, written by a Socialist, Franco Catalano, to the present century. "Storia d'Italia illustrata," published in Milan by Mondadori, includes a volume by Giacomo Perticone, *L'Italia contemporanea, 1871-1948* (Milan, 1962). The vast collection, "Storia d'Italia," edited by Ruggiero Romano and Corrado Vivanti (Turin: Giulio Einaudi editore, 1972 ff.), is written generally from a leftist perspective. It is organized rather cumbersomely on a thematic basis so that sometimes one must consult several volumes for a specific era. There is also a major synthesis, *Storia dell'Italia moderna* (Milan: Feltrinelli, 1956-78), written by Giorgio Candeloro, a Communist scholar. Volumes 7 and 8 cover the period 1896-1922; more are in preparation. *L'Italia del novecento*, 3 vols. (Rome: Biblioteca di storia patria, 1977), by the Marxist Salvatore F. Romano, is designed to serve as a textbook.

The 1870-1915 Era

The period from 1870 to 1915 has been viewed by many, though certainly not all, historians as an uninspired, prosaic era in Italian history. The excitement and romance of the Risorgimento had come to an end. The parliamentary system of the unified kingdom was not functioning very well, either under the Right or the Left, the two historic wings of Italian liberalism. Many of the nation's social problems were left unattended to while anticlerical politicians engaged instead in acrimonious disputes with the Vatican. The advent, however, of the industrial revolution in the North during the 1880s, followed by the founding of the Socialist party in 1892, opened the way for significant socioeconomic and political changes. These were interrupted in 1896 when the government of Francesco Crispi made an ill-advised attempt to conquer Ethiopia. The ensuing military debacle caused his government to fall, thus bringing to an end twenty years of rule by the Left. During the next few years there was repression and turmoil, climaxed by the assassination of King Umberto I by an anarchist in 1900.

The turn of the century saw a change for the better, so that the next fifteen years have come to be labeled Italy's "belle époque." The new spirit was associated to some degree with the advent of Victor Emmanuel III (1900-1946), for whom we now have a somewhat spotty biography by Silvio Bertoldi, *Vittorio Emanuele III* (Turin, 1971). But it is associated primarily with Giovanni Giolitti, the Piedmontese liberal who dominated most of the governments of that period. Under Giolitti the suffrage was democratized and a number of social and economic reforms were instituted. But there was also a less attractive side to Giolitti. He tolerated considerable political corruption and he allowed himself to be caught up in the campaign by the newly founded Nationalist Association for a war against the Turks in 1911-12, a war that was to bring Libya under Italy's control. In 1915 he was criticized for not speaking out against Italy's entry into the Great War. Finally, in 1921, he miscalculated badly when he worked out an electoral alliance with Mussolini's Fascists.

Though it is now somewhat outmoded, the classic study of this period is Benedetto Croce, *A History of Italy, 1871-1915* (Oxford, 1929), which looked upon the Giolittian era as the culmination of the best in Italian liberalism. The eminent Neapolitan historian and philosopher wrote this book for political reasons: he was determined to defend the liberal era which Gioacchino Volpe and other Fascist-oriented historians were denigrating.[6] In doing so, Croce almost certainly erred in the other direction. A cogent analysis of the conflicting interpretations of this era by Croce, Volpe, and others is presented by Leo Valiani, in *L'historiographie de l'Italie contemporaine* (Geneva, 1968).

Nino Valeri's *Giovanni Giolitti* (Turin, 1971) is the standard biography of the great Piedmontese statesman. Giolitti's own self-serving book, *Memoirs of My Life* (London, 1923; reprint, New York, 1973), has now been supplemented by the publication of three volumes of his correspondence, *Quarant'anni di politica italiana, dalle carte di Giovanni Giolitti* (Milan, 1962).

The "dean" of American specialists on Giolitti is A. William Salomone, author of *Italy in the Giolittian Era: Italian Democracy in the*

---

[6]Volpe wrote *Italia in cammino* in 1927. Later, he reworked it into a three-volume study, *Italia moderna, 1815-1915* (Florence, 1943-52).

13

Making (2d ed., Philadelphia, 1960), a brief, balanced analysis of political currents and thought. This book induced Gaetano Salvemini, who had previously been a sharp critic of Giolitti from the radical Left, to modify his assessment and concede that at least Giolitti was not as bad as Mussolini proved to be. Salomone has edited the anthology *Italy from the Risorgimento to Fascism: An Inquiry into the Origins of the Totalitarian State* (Garden City, N.Y., 1970) that gives a sampling of the divergent estimates of the Giolittian era. Salvatore Saladino has written a brief study, *Italy from Unification to 1919: Growth and Decay of a Liberal Regime* (New York, 1970), one-third of which focuses on the Giolittian period. John A. Thayer's book, *Italy and the Great War: Politics and Culture 1870-1915* (Madison, 1964), is passionately Crocean in spirit and full of insights into intellectual history. Among the younger writers to join the pro-Giolittian camp is Frank J. Coppa, whose book, *Planning, Protectionism, and Politics in Liberal Italy: Economics and Politics in the Giolittian Age* (Washington, 1971), concentrates upon the often neglected economic policies. Coppa perceives Giolitti to have been a practical statesman who was prepared to have the state take greater responsibility for the production of wealth and protection of its citizens.

Socialist politics of the late nineteenth and early twentieth century are analyzed in a recent book by Spencer Di Scala, *Dilemmas of Italian Socialism: The Politics of Filippo Turati* (Amherst, 1980). Di Scala's study of this "grand old man" of Italian democratic socialism is broader in scope than *Giolitti e Turati: Un incontro mancato* (Milan, 1976), by Brunello Vigezzi, which is the principal Italian work on this topic. Di Scala traces the splits within the Socialist party from its founding until the eve of the Great War. This is a topic that the Italian Socialist historian Gaetano Arfè has also dealt with in *Storia del socialismo italiano (1892-1926)* (Turin, 1965), and in a two-volume history of the Socialist party newspaper, *Storia dell'Avanti!* (Milan, 1956-58).

The newspaper press in the early twentieth century has attracted numerous other studies. Valerio Castronovo, *La stampa italiana dall'unità al fascismo* (Bari, 1973), provides excellent coverage of the subject. Luciana Frassati has undertaken a massive study, *Un uomo, un giornale: Alfredo Frassati,* Part I, 2 vols. (Rome, 1979), based on the correspondence of her father, the founder of Turin's *La Stampa* in 1897. Her study promises to be of signal importance for the history of both the Italian press and of the Giolittian period as a whole. Frassati was one of Giolitti's closest friends and staunchest supporters. Within ten years *La Stampa* became the principal rival in Italy of Luigi Albertini's Milan daily, *Il Corriere della Sera*. Ottavio Bariè has written a major biography, *Luigi Albertini (1871-1941)* (Turin, 1972), which points out, among other things, that Albertini favored intervention in the Great War in 1915, whereas Frassati appealed for a policy of "vigilant neutrality." In Rome, meanwhile, Luigi Cesana established (1878) the newspaper *Il Messaggero*. Giuseppe Talamo has begun a history of its first century of publication: *Il "Messaggero" e la sua città: Cento anni di storia*, Vol. I, *1878-1918* (Florence, 1979). This latter newspaper quickly became more conservative than either *La Stampa* or *Corriere della Sera*. By 1915 it passed into the hands of the Perrone brothers of the Ansaldo industry. In 1925 the Fascist dictatorship deprived both Frassati and Albertini of their newspapers; thereafter, these papers and a number of others came increasingly under the domination of such industrial giants as the Agnellis, the Crespis, and the Perrones. It is ironic that it should have been Mussolini, one of the outstanding political journalists of the twentieth century, who dealt the deathblow to Italy's independent press. His absurd slogan was to be "the Italian press is a free press because it is a Fascist press."

Pioneering work in Catholic historiography with respect to the turn of the century era includes studies by Gabriele De Rosa, *Storia del movimento cattolico in Italia*, 2 vols. (Bari, 1966); Fausto Fonzi, *I cattolici e la società italiana dopo l'unità* (Milan, 1953); Giovanni Spadolini, *Giolitti e i cattolici (1901-1914)* (Florence, 1960); and Pietro Scoppola, *Crisi modernista e rinnovamento cattolico in Italia* (Bologna, 1961), dealing with the Modernist heresy of the early 1900s. An Italian priest who served as the *éminence grise* behind the campaign of Pope Pius X (1903-14) against the Modernist current was Mgr. Umberto Benigni. His secretive work, which was followed by blatant support for Fascism until his death in 1934, has recently been explored by the French sociologist Émile Poulat, *Catholicisme, démocratie et socialisme: Le mouvement catholique et Mgr Benigni de la naissance du socialisme a la victoire du fascisme* (Paris, 1977).

Foreign Policy and Overseas Expansion, 1900-1919

Those who seek more details regarding Italian foreign policy from 1870 to 1925 than Christopher Seton-Watson provides in his admirable book mentioned above can now turn to Richard J. B. Bosworth, *Italy: The Least of the Great Powers. Italian Foreign Policy Before the First World War* (London, 1979). Three-quarters of this Australian scholar's lengthy tome cover 1910-14 and focus especially on the foreign policy of the Sicilian Marchese Antonino di San Giuliano. Bosworth finds little in Italian diplomacy to praise; indeed, he concludes that it often produced policy which was not only ambivalent and tortuous but, in the final analysis, crudely dishonest. Nor does he think that Italian imperialism was the product of economic motives. A still more heavily documented account is Brunello Vigezzi's massive work, *L'Italia di fronte alla prima guerra mondiale*, Vol. I: *L'Italia neutrale* (Milan, 1966). On the foreign policy of the period 1870-1896 the classic Italian analysis is Federico Chabod, *Storia della politica estera italiana dal 1870 al 1896: Le premesse* (Bari, 1951), which explains brilliantly the persistent themes or "premises."

Industrial Imperialism, 1908-1915 (Berkeley, 1975), by Richard A. Webster, studies Italian aspirations in the Balkans and Asia Minor in those years. Webster claims that Italian imperialism was essentially industrial in this period, centering on ports, railways, and mining projects. The "population-outlet gambit" was only propaganda. He contends that most of the industrial sectors of the Italian economy, and the banks which financed them, owed their creation and growth to close links with the state. It was structural "economic imbalance," produced by late, rapid industrialization, that motivated Italian "industrial imperialism." A restless and adventurous spirit entered Italy's foreign policy after 1911. Italy was not an exporter of capital, but her export needs in the area of industrial goods, systems and skills, technical and even entrepreneurial, explain her drive for exclusive colonial space, he argues.

More recently, Webster has shifted his attention to the subsequent period in two long articles, "La tecnocrazia italiana e i sistemi industriali verticali: Il caso dell'Ansaldo (1914-1921)," *Storia contemporanea* 9 (Apr. 1978): 205-40, and "Una speranza rinviata: L'espansione industriale italiana e il problema del petrolio dopo la prima guerra mondiale," *Storia contemporanea* 11 (Apr. 1980): 219-

81. In the latter study Webster examines how it was that Italy failed to develop into an industrial power of world rank. The economist Jon S. Cohen has recently written *Finance and Industrialization in Italy, 1894-1914* (New York, 1977).

On the subject of Italian imperialism in Libya there are two major studies in English. William C. Askew, *Europe and Italy's Acquisition of Libya, 1911-12* (Durham, N.C., 1942), concentrates on the diplomacy surrounding this war which Giolitti undertook, somewhat against his better judgment, on the fiftieth anniversary of Italian unification. A broader study is *Fourth Shore: The Italian Colonization of Libya* (Chicago, 1975), by Claudio G. Segrè. Written on the basis of archival research and interviews, this is a lucid book that clarifies the complex story of Italy's conflicting policies and aspirations with respect to that sector of North Africa. The author contends that Italy acquired this region for political rather than economic motives. It was not until 1921 that the financier Giuseppe Volpi[7] set out to develop Libya along the lines he had practiced in Montenegro and projected for Asia Minor, i.e., by private capitalist enterprise employing indigenous labor. The role of the state was to be confined to the provision of cheap land (expropriated from the natives) and fiscal advantages. Only with the appointment of Italo Balbo as governor in 1934 did large-scale colonization begin. Balbo was no capitalist; first and foremost, he was a flamboyant Fascist "man of action."[8] His aim was to settle half a million people in Libya by 1950. Actually, by 1940 the figure had reached only 110,000—representing but 12% of the total Libyan population—and those Italians soon found themselves stranded when Libya became a battlefield in World War II. Libya did not provide a solution to the land hunger and overpopulation of Italy's Mezzogiorno because the great majority of the colonists came from the North. Segrè also points out that the nationality law of 1939 was clearly racist in spirit, keeping the Arabs in second-class citizenship. By 1970, those Italian settlers

[7]Sergio Romano, an Italian diplomat, has published a study of this entrepreneur: *Giuseppe Volpi: Industria e finanza tra Giolitti e Mussolini* (Milan, 1979).

[8]Giorgio Rochat has written a good study of the earlier activities of Balbo, who had started out as a Fascist *squadrista* in Ferrara: *Italo Balbo, aviatore e ministro dell'aeronautica, 1926-1933* (Bologna, 1979). Later, Balbo fell from favor with Mussolini. He was killed in an airplane crash over Tobruk in June 1940. For these later years see the article by Claudio G. Segrè, "Fascism as Fiefdoms: Balbo, Mussolini and the Totalitarian State," *Cesare Barbieri Courier: A Special Issue on Mussolini and Italian Fascism* (Hartford, 1980), pp. 36-41.

who had not already packed up and moved out were expelled by the radical nationalists of the new Libyan republic.

Using archival sources and writing from a socialist perspective, Romain Rainero is the author of *La rivendicazione fascista sulla Tunisia* (Milan, 1978), which covers the story of some 100,000 Italian colonists in that sector of North Africa between 1868 and 1965. Rainero emphasizes the inconsistencies in Mussolini's policies toward the French protectorate. His earlier book, *L'anticolonialismo italiano da Assab ad Adua* (Milan, 1971), dealt with the situation in Eritrea from 1869 to 1896.

Robert L. Hess, *Italian Colonialism in Somalia* (Chicago, 1966), is a study of a section of east Africa that became a center of Italian commercial activity after 1889 and, to one degree or another, was to remain under Italian tutelage until 1960. The Fascist era brought large-scale investments of capital into Somalia, but the colony never became a paying proposition. After the Italian invasion of Ethiopia in 1935–36, Somalia was merged into Italian East Africa.

L'emigrazione italiana dall'unità alla seconda guerra mondiale (Bologna, 1979), by Ercole Sori, is a lengthy demographic study of almost a century of Italian emigration. *Italian Immigrants Abroad: A Bibliography on the Italian Experience Outside Italy in Europe, the Americas, Australia, and Africa* (Detroit, 1979), edited by Vittorio Briani with a supplement by Francesco Cordasco, is a handy guide. There is a rapidly expanding literature on Italian Americans but it cannot be dealt with here.

On Italy's role in the Great War, Seton-Watson's book offers the best coverage in English, while Luigi Albertini, *Origins of the War of 1914*, 3 vols. (London, 1952), continues to be one of the most reliable studies of the general diplomatic background. Albertini had turned to writing diplomatic history after the Fascists ousted him in 1925 from the directorate of his newspaper, *Il Corriere della Sera*. John Whittam's book, *The Politics of the Italian Army, 1861–1918* (Hamden, Conn., 1977), treats the period from Italian unification through the Great War. It is descriptive rather than analytical and is based on secondary sources. Despite these limitations, it is of some usefulness.

In their own discussion of the Great War, Italian writers have not given much concern to the struggle as a whole. Instead, they have riveted their attention on the circumstances of Italian intervention, the Caporetto crisis of 1917, and the question of why the protracted conflict led to the breakdown of the old liberal governing class, thus opening the door to Fascism. There is now general agreement that most of the country preferred neutrality but that the three principal neutralist forces (Giolittians, Socialists, and Catholics) failed because they were paralyzed by mutual distrust. Nino Valeri has explored this theme in various studies. A distinguished military historian, Piero Pieri, discusses the war itself in *L'Italia nella prima guerra mondiale* (4th ed., Turin, 1971). Two important recent books on the period include the eighth volume (dealing with 1914-1922) of the Communist historian Giorgio Candeloro's *Storia dell'Italia moderna* (Milan, 1979) and the non-Marxist writer Piero Melograni's *Storia politica della grande guerra, 1915-1918* (Bari, 1969). Despite its title, this latter book focuses more on the psychological and socio-economic dimensions of the war in Italy than on the political aspects.[9] Melograni ignores almost completely wartime diplomacy and the purely military, strategic aspects of the conflict, but on the themes that he does treat he is fair. The author argues that the Caporetto debacle was caused less by a breakdown in morale than by strictly military factors. Alberto Monticone, *Gli Italiani in uniforme, 1915-1918: Intellettuali, borghesi e disertori* (Bari, 1975), is an informative social history. Giorgio Rochat, a well-informed Marxist specialist in military history, suggests new possibilities for research in his manual, *L'Italia nella prima guerra mondiale: Problemi di interpretazione e prospettive di ricerca* (Milan, 1976). Louis J. Nigro's "Propaganda, Politics, and the New Diplomacy: The Impact of Wilsonian Propaganda on Politics and Public Opinion in Italy, 1917-1919" (unpublished PhD dissertation, Vanderbilt University, 1979) sheds some new light on the Wilsonian phenomenon in Italy during the last phase of the war. The classic study of the social and economic effects of the war is Luigi Einaudi, *La condotta economica e gli effetti sociali della guerra italiana* (Bari, 1933). Much more needs to be done, however, in clarifying how the war reshaped Italian society and political culture and thus gave rise to the mentality called Fascism.

René Albrecht-Carrié's *Italy at the Paris Peace Conference* (New York, 1938) remains the standard treatment of that conclave, which saw the first serious clash between Italy and the United States. The

---

[9]On the role of political parties and public opinion during the war there are good papers by Vittorio De Caprariis and Leo Valiani, printed respectively in the *Atti* of the 41st and 44th congresses on the history of the Italian Risorgimento (Rome: Istituto per la storia del Risorgimento italiano, 1965 and 1970).

desire of many Italians to acquire Fiume, even though this Adriatic seaport had not been promised to them in the secret Treaty of London of 1915, lay at the heart of this crisis. Ivo Lederer, *Yugoslavia at the Paris Peace Conference* (New Haven, 1964), presents the Fiume conflict from a different perspective and on the basis of more recent scholarship.

The hidden papers of the Italian diplomat Sidney Sonnino, who was minister of foreign affairs (1914-19) and attended the Paris Peace Conference in 1919, were discovered in a back room of a Tuscan villa a few years ago by an American historian, Benjamin F. Brown. At his urging, the complete works of Sonnino are being published jointly in Italy (by Laterza of Bari) and in this country (University of Kansas Press, Lawrence, 1972 ff.).

A number of studies of Italy's postwar policy regarding the Adriatic have been published by Paolo Alatri, *Nitti, D'Annunzio e la questione adriatica* (Milan, 1959); Renzo De Felice, *D'Annunzio politico, 1918-1938* (Bari, 1978); and others. In English there is a study by Michael A. Ledeen, *The First Duce: D'Annunzio at Fiume* (Baltimore, 1977), which seeks to present a major revision of our view of the Fiume adventure. Ledeen argues that the poet-condottiere D'Annunzio was one of the modern world's "great innovators" in the field of mass psychology and that his occupation of Fiume in 1919-20 was therefore "one of the twentieth century's major watersheds." Ledeen emphasizes D'Annunzio's genius for style, pointing out that it was he who invented the balcony harangues and ritualistic gestures that were later adopted by Mussolini. The author insists, nevertheless, that despite the common rituals, the social and political vision of D'Annunzio remained qualitatively different from that of Mussolini. In any case, it is clear that Italy's political stage was too small for two such prima donnas. D'Annunzio had to be content with the sonorous title of Prince of the Snowy Mountain and retirement to a villa on Lake Garda, where he died in 1938. Ledeen's major contribution is the light he sheds on the neglected second period (1920) of the Fiume adventure, when such leftist supporters as the syndicalist Alceste De Ambris had their day. Other books that offer some insights are Anthony Rhodes, *D'Annunzio: The Poet as Superman* (New York, 1959), and Philippe Jullian, *D'Annunzio* (New York, 1972), the latter translated from the French. Paolo Alatri is writing a biography of D'Annunzio that will appear in the biographical series "La vita sociale della nuova Italia," directed by Nino Valeri (Turin: UTET). Emiliana P. Noether has written a discerning essay, "Mussolini and D'Annunzio, A Strange Friendship," in *Cesare Barbieri Courier: A Special Issue on Mussolini and Italian Fascism* (Hartford, 1980), pp. 50-63.

The Fascist Era, 1919-1945: General Works

In March 1919 Mussolini (1883-1945), a maverick ex-Socialist and editor of *Il Popolo d'Italia,* organized in Milan his movement of "fighting Fascists." His Blackshirt followers were made up at first chiefly of ultranationalistic war veterans and youth, ex-syndicalists, ex-socialists, Futurists (including Filippo Marinetti), and lower-middle-class elements who felt the country was threatened by bolshevism and that this would lower their own socioeconomic status. Many of the workers and peasants in the North were in a revolutionary mood at war's end because of the strains and divisions brought on by the prolonged conflict and by the heady news of Russia's Bolshevik Revolution. The introduction of proportional representation, combined with universal manhood suffrage and large electoral districts, had opened the way for an entirely new postwar political structure. The Catholics, under the leadership of the Sicilian priest Luigi Sturzo, entered the political arena in 1919 with a new Partito Popolare Italiano (PPI) that quickly won 100 seats in the Chamber. The Socialist party's ranks swelled, making it the largest party in the country. The high point of Socialist and labor agitation occurred in the late summer of 1920 when metallurgical workers occupied plants in the northern cities. Eventually, however, these strikers had to reach accommodation with the owners on the latter's terms. The revolutionary tide now turned. Disillusioned left-wing extremists seceded from the main trunk of socialism to organize their separate Italian Communist Party (PCI) in January 1921, while on the opposite side a revisionist Socialist party (PSU) under Filippo Turati and Giacomo Matteotti emerged. Meanwhile, the Fascists spread out from their base in Milan to win wide support among landowners in the lower Po valley who were determined to suppress the new Socialist and Catholic peasant organizations. "Agrarian" Fascism, led by such armed *squadristi* as Dino Grandi and Italo Balbo, presented a challenge to Mussolini's leadership of the party but he managed to hang on to it. Virtual civil war characterized the period until 1922, with the Fascists now clearly in the ascendancy. Mussolini quickly shed his earlier republican rhetoric and openly courted the King, the Army, and the Church. One weak liberal government after another collapsed.

At last on October 28, 1922, when the Fascists were calling for a "march on Rome," Victor Emmanuel III invited the Duce of Fascism to form a coalition government. At first the Fascists held only a minority of the portfolios. Premier Mussolini had to wait until after the assassination of Giacomo Matteotti in June 1924, and his surmounting of the ensuing six-months parliamentary crisis (the "Aventine" secession), before he was able to establish the dictatorship. Prodded by the "revolt of the party consuls," Mussolini carried out a coup d'état on January 3, 1925, and by November 1926 succeeded in nailing down the so-called totalitarian state. By that time, all non-Fascist parties were dissolved, as were the non-Fascist labor syndicates. Censorship was imposed. A secret police and a Special Tribunal for the Defense of the State were established. Many of the opposition leaders were either arrested or harried from the land. The regime was ultranationalistic and imperialistic. It had its own party Militia. Though elitist in its hierarchical structure, it differed markedly from old-fashioned military and authoritarian regimes by its conscious mobilization and indoctrination of the masses. Private property and capitalism were preserved but there was much governmental intervention in the economy. Parliament was emasculated. The Chamber of Deputies was replaced in due course by the Chamber of Fasces and Corporations, which represented the single party and functional rather than either numerical or geographical constituencies. Only a few elements of the old system remained: the King (who still claimed the allegiance of the regular army), the appointive and docile Senate, and the Roman Catholic Church. Victor Emmanuel III was quite willing to collaborate with Fascism in a kind of "dyarchy" system, while Pope Pius XI (1922–1939) was happy to give formal recognition to the Fascist State in the Lateran pacts of February 11, 1929.

The first full-dress study of the entire span of Fascism appeared in 1952 when Luigi Salvatorelli and Giovanni Mira brought out their *Storia del fascismo,* which in subsequent editions was retitled *Storia d'Italia nel periodo fascista* (3rd ed., Turin, 1964). Unfortunately, it has never been translated. Salvatorelli was a distinguished liberal historian, while his collaborator was a well-informed journalist who was knowledgeable in economics.[10] Although they did not have access to the official archives, they succeeded in writing a very factual, perceptive, and comprehensive account drawn from a wide range of sources. The counterpart of their book, written from the Fascist angle, is Attilio Tamaro, *Venti anni di storia, 1922-1943*, 3 vols. (Rome, 1971), dealing with the heyday of the regime, and his supplementary *Due anni di storia, 1943-1945*, 3 vols. (Rome, 1948-50), focusing on the curious epilogue to it, the Italian Social Republic in the German-occupied northern half of the peninsula.

A short but excellent work that is available in English is *A History of Italian Fascism* (London, 1963), written by the distinguished liberal historian, Federico Chabod. Based on a series of lectures he was invited to deliver at the Sorbonne in 1950, it covers not only the Fascist era but the post-World War II reconstruction. Chabod had participated in the Armed Resistance of 1943-45 in his native Val d'Aosta. After the war he became director of Croce's new Istituto italiano per gli studi storici in Naples, where he exerted a powerful influence on a generation of young Italian and foreign scholars. He was honored by election to the presidency of the XI International Congress of the Historical Sciences before his untimely death in 1960.[11]

Other brief but cogent discussions in English of the Fascist era include H. Stuart Hughes's book mentioned earlier; Alan Cassels, *Fascism* (New York, 1975); Elizabeth Wiskemann, *Fascism in Italy: Its Development and Influence* (London, 1969); and S. William Halperin, *Mussolini and Italian Fascism* (Princeton, 1964). Charles F. Delzell, ed., *Mediterranean Fascism, 1919-1945* (New York, 1970), deals chiefly with Italy and contains many illustrative documents with commentary. An important Italian Marxist interpretation is Enzo Santarelli's two-volume *Storia del movimento e del regime fascista* (Rome, 1967). It is a more restrained and nuanced treatment than was true of most Communist writings on the subject during the Stalinist era.

---

[10]For an assessment of Salvatorelli's many historical works, see Charles F. Delzell's introductory essay to Salvatorelli, *The Risorgimento: Thought and Action* (New York, 1970).

[11]A. William Salomone has written an appreciative essay on Chabod in *Historians of Modern Europe*, ed. Hans Schmitt (Baton Rouge, 1971). This festschrift in honor of S. William Halperin, another specialist on Italy, also contains essays on the Italian historians Gioacchino Volpe, Gaetano Salvemini, and Adolfo Omodeo. These were contributed, respectively, by Edward R. Tannenbaum, George T. Peck, and Charles F. Delzell.

Philip V. Cannistraro, with the help of scholars from several countries, has compiled a reference work, *A Historical Dictionary of Fascism* (Westport, Conn., 1981). Assisted by others, Frank J. Coppa is compiling for the same publisher (Greenwood Press) a companion volume, *Dictionary of Modern Italian History*.

Biographies of Mussolini and Other Fascists

Many writers have approached Italian Fascism through biographies of its Duce.[12] This is understandable, since the regime can scarcely be envisaged without the presence of its colorful and charismatic leader. Certainly Mussolini played a major role in shaping foreign policy, but whether he always took the lead in the field of domestic affairs is more debatable. In the latter area, a strong case can be made that he acted chiefly as an arbiter among contesting pressure groups.

The most readable one-volume biographies of Mussolini have been produced outside of Italy. Of these the most important is Sir Ivone Kirkpatrick, *Mussolini: A Study in Power* (New York, 1964). It has stood up well, especially in its coverage of the period before 1929 and in its shrewd analysis of Mussolini's personality. The last part is more derivative, drawing upon the studies of foreign policy by Elizabeth Wiskemann and Sir F. William Deakin. Kirkpatrick was a British diplomat who had opportunities to observe Mussolini over a considerable span of time.

Among the shorter biographies designed for the general public, mention should be made of *Mussolini* (Chicago, 1961), by Laura Fermi, the Jewish widow of the émigré Italian nuclear physicist, Enrico Fermi. She admits that it was not until the late 1930s that she came to recognize the flaws in the Duce's character. She is quite selective in her choice of topics and goes in for considerable psychological analysis. Less satisfactory and uneven in their coverage are the popular accounts written by Christopher Hibbert, Richard Collier, and Roy MacGregor-Hastie. For those who enjoy reading about Mussolini's sex life as well as about the ludicrous aspects of his regime, one can turn to *Mussolini: An Intimate Life* (London, 1953), a sprightly volume by the well-informed Italian journalist Paolo Monelli which has been translated into English. A French historian, Max Gallo, wrote a popular history in 1964 that keeps Mussolini at

---

[12]For a partial listing, see Charles F. Delzell, "Benito Mussolini: A Guide to the Biographical Literature," *Journal of Modern History* 35 (Dec. 1963): 339–53.

center stage. The English version is *Mussolini's Italy: Twenty Years of the Fascist Era* (New York, 1973). The principal Italian apologia for the Duce is the detailed biography, *Mussolini: L'uomo e l'opera*, 4 vols. (3rd ed., Florence, 1963), by the Fascist journalists, Giorgio Pini and Duilio Susmel.

An exhaustive, archive-based Italian biography is now in progress by Renzo De Felice of the University of Rome. He has emerged as that country's leading specialist on Fascism. Thus far, his massive study boasts four thick tomes published between 1965 and 1974: *Mussolini il rivoluzionario, 1883-1920; Mussolini il fascista: La conquista del potere, 1921-1925; Mussolini il fascista: L'organizzazione dello Stato fascista, 1925-1929;* and *Mussolini il duce: Gli anni del consenso, 1929-1936* (Turin, 1965-74). The remaining two volumes will be labeled *Mussolini il duce: Lo Stato totalitario, 1936-1939;* and *L'Alleato, 1939-1945*. Unfortunately, none of this opus has yet been translated into English. De Felice's work has long since ceased to be a mere biography; rather it has become a history of Italian Fascism on a giant scale. It is characterized more by a succession of documents than by either interpretation or narration. No volume contains fewer than 600 pages, and one runs to 950. The author's sentences are often so convoluted and interspersed with parenthetical digressions that they remain afloat for almost a page. De Felice concedes that some of his judgments are tentative, and he has not hesitated to modify them as he has gone along. He promises to write a one-volume summary when he finishes his mammoth project.

It is hardly surprising that in a politically polarized country like Italy the appearance of each installment of this great work has stirred controversy. A number of critics have charged that the author is not really so objective as he claims to be, and that he has been too lenient toward Mussolini. Certain Marxist critics have been especially hostile to De Felice's challenges to their orthodoxies. Some of them questioned the appropriateness of labeling the first volume "Mussolini the Revolutionary," especially in light of his lack of moral fibre and his maverick role after being expelled from the editorship of the Socialist party newspaper *Avanti!* in the autumn of 1914. By the time the fourth tome, subtitled "The Years of Consensus, 1929-1936," appeared, a veritable storm of protest erupted. In that volume De Felice argued that in the years from the Lateran pacts until the end of the Ethiopian War, Mussolini enjoyed a tenuous consensus of genuine support from Italians. It rested largely upon his charisma, the regime's new accommodation with the Church, the country's emergence from the Depression, the launching of new social programs, and the gaining of prestige during the Ethiopian struggle. De Felice conceded that this "consensus" proved to be ephemeral, especially after the Duce's intervention in the Spanish Civil War and his announcement of the Rome-Berlin Axis in 1936, both of which were unpopular moves at home.

For several months some veterans of the anti-Fascist struggle and subscribers to its "mythology" were outraged by De Felice's "consensus" theory. They insisted that he pictured greater mass support for the Duce than was really the case. They also questioned the generally favorable marks he gave to Mussolini in handling the international complications of the Ethiopian War. And some of them declared that De Felice allowed himself at times to be taken in by propaganda in the Fascist documents and failed to take equal measure of evidence from opposition sources. But when one prominent Communist veteran of the anti-Fascist struggle, Giorgio Amendola, came to De Felice's defense, much of the storm subsided.

Meanwhile, De Felice responded vigorously to the charges in a long interview that he granted to the American historian Michael A. Ledeen. First published in Italy in 1975, this interview has since come out in English as Renzo De Felice, *Fascism: An Informal Introduction to its Theory and Practice,* ed. Michael A. Ledeen, (New Brunswick, N.J., 1976).[13] Some of the statements in this interview have opened the way for further questions to be put to the Italian scholar, particularly with respect to his suggestion that "fascism was . . . the attempt of the [petty] bourgeoisie in its ascendancy—not in crisis—to assert itself as a new class, a new force . . . against both the bourgeoisie and the proletariat." In the earlier volumes of his biography De Felice had contended, like Luigi Salvatorelli in *Nazionalfascismo* (Turin, 1923), Guido Dorso in *La rivoluzione meridionale* (Turin, 1925), and most other historians, that Mussolini's successful rise to power owed much to the support he received from a lower middle class that feared displacement and proletarianization

---

[13]De Felice also clarified his points in a radio interview in 1977 with George R. Urban, ed., *Eurocommunism: Its Roots and Failure in Italy and Elsewhere* (New York, 1978), Ch. 5. See also Michael A. Ledeen, "Renzo De Felice and the Controversy over Italian Fascism," *Journal of Contemporary History* 11 (Oct. 1976): 269-82.

in a time of crisis. De Felice, in his interview with Ledeen, did not entirely deny this point but argued that these people were only "fringe" elements. He declared that he had documentation from the papers of local Fascist groups to prove his new contention that most of the lower middle class were really ascending under Fascism rather than being squeezed downward into proletarianization.

Several critics have also expressed doubts that the validity of the sharp distinctions De Felice has made between Italian Fascism as a "movement" and as a "regime." The author has contended that Italian Fascism as a "movement" or as an "ideal" was a "positive" and "vital force" for renovation, for transformation of the country, but he is ready to concede that Fascism as a "regime," or as a "reality," was both "oppressive" and "repressive." In his view, the "regime" rested upon Mussolini's calculated compromises with capitalism, the monarchy, the old leading classes, the bureaucracy, and the Church. The "movement" or "ideal," on the other hand, was born of a "revolutionary" protest against such compromises. The Fascist "movement" represented an example of major change or "fracture" in Italian history, whereas the "regime" was another example of "continuity" in that nation's history. According to De Felice, the differences between "movement" and "regime" were not chronologically distinct but continued as rival tendencies within Fascism. Mussolini was the "unifying thread, the element of synthesis," the "arbiter" of the two tendencies. (pp. 42-45, 52).

What about biographies of other prominent Italians in the era of Fascism? Italy, unhappily, does not have a strong literary tradition in the genre of biography, but Nino Valeri has endeavored to remedy this deficiency by commissioning an impressive biographical series, "La vita sociale della nuova Italia" (Turin: UTET), now well on the way to completion. The series calls for lengthy biographies of forty prominent figures in the political, socioeconomic, cultural, and intellectual life of Italy since its unification. The fact that Valeri decided to include only two Fascist hierarchs in the series—*Benito Mussolini,* published by Gaspare Giudice in 1969, and *Giuseppe Bottai,* in preparation by Francesco Sirugo— tells us something about his low regard for Fascism's enduring impact upon the social life of the new Italy.

On a considerably more modest scale, Ferdinando Cordova has recently edited a readable volume, *Uomini e volti del fascismo* (Rome,

1980), that contains succinct profiles of fourteen hierarchs: Italo Balbo, Michele Bianchi, Arturo Bocchini, Giuseppe Bottai, Galeazzo Ciano, Emilio De Bono, Roberto Farinacci, Luigi Federzoni, Alfredo Rocco, Edmondo Rossoni, Arrigo Serpieri, Achille Starace, Augusto Turati, and Giuseppe Volpi. The essays were written by Italian, American, and British specialists. Stuart J. Woolf is the author of the concluding chapter, "Fascism and its hierarchs."

The Rise of Italian Fascism

A significant body of literature is emerging on the rise of Italian Fascism and on its prewar ideological background. The classic study is *The Rise of Italian Fascism, 1918-1922* (London, 1938), by Angelo Tasca, a political exile who was then writing under the pseudonym of "A. Rossi." Tasca was one of the founders of the Italian Communist party in 1921 but was expelled in the early 1930s, at which point he became a Socialist. Tasca's book carefully analyzes the political maneuverings of that period. The author is especially well informed on the actions of the Socialists, Communists, and organized labor. After World War II, Tasca brought out an enlarged Italian edition, *Nascita e avvento del fascismo: L'Italia dal 1918 al 1922* (Florence, 1950).

Because of his outspoken hostility to the regime, Gaetano Salvemini was ousted from his professorship of history at the University of Florence, deprived of his citizenship, and forced to flee the country in 1925. Federico Chabod guided him surreptitiously across the mountainous frontier. Salvemini received an appointment as Lecturer at Harvard University, where he taught for many years and wrote a number of polemical books attacking Mussolini's dictatorship.[14] One of the best of these was based on a course he offered in 1942 that dealt with the decade 1919-1929. It was published posthumously in Italy in 1961 and later in the original English text as *The Origins of Fascism in Italy* (New York, 1973), with an introduction by Roberto Vivarelli, who is editing Salvemini's collected works.

Vivarelli is himself the author of a major study, *Il dopoguerra in*

---

[14]Salvemini's recollections of his activities abroad are fascinating: *Memorie di un fuoruscito*, ed. Gaetano Arfè (Milan, 1960). There is a rather hostile biography by Gaspare De Caro, *Gaetano Salvemini* (Turin, 1970). On his activities in Italian politics before the Great War, there is a major study by Hugo Bütler, *Gaetano Salvemini und die italienische Politik vor dem Ersten Weltkrieg* (Tübingen, 1978).

Italia e l'avvento del fascismo (1918-1922), of which only the first volume has thus far appeared: *Dalla fine della guerra all'impresa di Fiume* (Naples, 1967). Written under the encouragement of Chabod, whose historical institute in Naples published it, Vivarelli's book stands very much in the Salveminian tradition of democratic radicalism. The author takes issue with several of De Felice's contentions regarding the supposedly leftist orientation of Fascism "of the first hour." Vivarelli has also written a perspicacious review-article, "Italy 1919-21: The Current State of Research," *Journal of Contemporary History* 3 (Jan. 1968): 103-112.

The most up-to-date and thorough study of Fascism's initial decade is the meticulously researched volume by the Oxford scholar, Adrian Lyttelton, *The Seizure of Power: Fascism in Italy 1919-1929* (New York, 1973). Lyttelton has drawn extensively on unpublished archival sources and periodical literature as well as on Italian research to illuminate previously unexplored areas of his subject. He emphasizes that the Fascist seizure of power neither began nor ended with the March on Rome in October 1922. It was achieved rather by a gradual subversion of the liberal order and involved not only the destruction of all political opposition but also the creation of new institutions designed to control economic and cultural life. The evolution of the Fascist party and its changing relationship with the Italian State is Lyttelton's central theme. Totalitarianism—a term that Mussolini coined—remained more of an aspiration than an actual achievement, but the system of controls created by the Fascists did anticipate in some ways the more rigid ones set up in Nazi Germany.

A number of writers have looked into the prewar antecedents of Italian Fascism, paying special attention to Mussolini's possible links with the syndicalists, as well as to the factors that induced some of these syndicalists to shift toward a nationalist position during the Great War. The earliest scholar to explore this problem was the American, Gaudens Megaro, whose *Mussolini in the Making* (Boston, 1938) dealt with Mussolini's career up to the time of his expulsion from the Socialist party in 1914. Megaro emphasized that Fascism was ideologically an amalgam of the doctrines of nationalism and syndicalism. In his research in Italy, which was undertaken with considerable difficulty during the years of the dictatorship, Megaro managed to unearth amusing facts about young Mussolini's socialist and antimilitarist past that the Duce later carefully tried to keep concealed. This period of Mussolini's life has also been explored in detail, as noted above, in the first volume of De Felice's massive biography.

More recently, several American scholars have been probing into the syndicalist dimension of Mussolini's early career. David D. Roberts has written *The Syndicalist Tradition and Italian Fascism* (Chapel Hill, 1979), while A. James Gregor has published *Young Mussolini and the Intellectual Origins of Fascism* (Berkeley, 1979). Roberts, a historian, is more restrained in his contentions than is Gregor, a political scientist. The latter propounds a startling revisionist thesis that Mussolini was not an opportunistic demagogue but a truly coherent and consistent political philosopher. Both authors are keen on relating the thought of Mussolini to such syndicalist writers as Robert Michels, Angelo O. Olivetti, and Sergio Panunzio. All three of these syndicalists were influenced, in turn, by the French mythmaker and author of *Reflections on Violence* (1908), Georges Sorel, who, at the age of seventy-five, died two months before the Fascist March on Rome. With respect to Sorel, the most recent exegesis is Jack J. Roth, *The Cult of Violence: Sorel and the Sorelians* (Berkeley, 1980), which analyzes the four successive movements that he was interested in: revolutionary syndicalism, integral nationalism, Bolshevism, and Fascism.[15] The eagerness of Gregor and Roberts to underscore the syndicalist connection runs a risk of slighting the importance of other writers on Mussolini—for example, Gustave Le Bon and Friedrich Nietzsche—who may have been even more influential. Gregor thinks that Megaro erred in asserting that Mussolini did not yet hold nationalist views in 1909 when he lived in the Austrian Trentino. Gregor finds phrases here and there in Mussolini's *Collected Works*[16] that prove, at least to his

[15] See also Roth's article, "The Roots of Italian Fascism: Sorel and Sorelismo," *Journal of Modern History* 39 (Mar. 1967): 30–45. Other major studies include James H. Meisel, *The Genesis of Georges Sorel: An Account of His Formative Period Followed by a Study of His Influence* (Ann Arbor, 1951); Richard Humphrey, *Georges Sorel: Prophet Without Honor: A Study in Anti-Intellectualism* (Cambridge, Mass., 1951); Scott H. Lytle, "Georges Sorel: Apostle of Fanaticism," *Modern France: Problems of the Third and Fourth Republics*, ed. Edward Mead Earle (Princeton, 1951), pp. 264–90; and H. Stuart Hughes's chapter, "Georges Sorel's Search for Reality," in his *Consciousness and Society: The Reorientation of European Social Thought, 1890–1930*, rev. ed. (New York, 1977).

[16] *Opera omnia di Benito Mussolini*, 42 vols., ed. Edoardo and Duilio Susmel (Florence, 1951–63 and Rome, 1980).

satisfaction, that Mussolini was becoming a patriotic Italian nationalist even in those early years.

Nationalism was probably even more important than syndicalism in the ideological mix which resulted in Fascism. Here Alexander J. De Grand's *The Italian Nationalist Association* (Lincoln, 1978) makes a distinct contribution. He demonstrates, on the basis of the family papers of Luigi Federzoni and other archives, that the Italian Nationalist political movement, as elaborated after 1903 by Enrico Corradini, Federzoni, and Alfredo Rocco, was eventually to steer Fascism in the direction of traditional conservative authoritarianism. The conservative Nationalists were so well organized economically and politically that they quickly succeeded by the mid-1920s in exercising decisive control over the Fascist party, thereby limiting its radical possibilities. Among the major Italian studies of the Nationalists are Paolo Ungari's brilliant *Alfredo Rocco e l'ideologia giuridica del fascismo* (Brescia, 1963); Franco Gaeta, *Nazionalismo italiano* (Naples, 1965); and Francesco Perfetti, *Il nazionalismo italiano dalle origini alla fusione col fascismo* (Bologna, 1977). Mention should also be made of Emilio Gentile's study, *Le origini dell'ideologia fascista (1918-1925)* (Bari, 1975).

The anthology, *Italian Fascisms: From Pareto to Gentile,* ed. Adrian Lyttelton (London, 1973), provides a useful collection of texts that illustrate the "philosophical" views of Mussolini, Corradini, Rocco, D'Annunzio, Giuseppe Prezzolini, Vilfredo Pareto, Giovanni Papini, Ardengo Soffici, Agostino Lanzillo, Filippo Marinetti, and Giovanni Gentile.

Regional Studies of Fascism

Regional studies of Fascism are now in vogue. A first-rate monograph by an English scholar, Paul Corner, *Fascism in Ferrara 1915-1925* (London, 1975), offers a model for this kind of history. Corner underscores the special character of the new capitalist, agrarian economy of the lower Po valley around Ferrara that enabled Fascist Blackshirts like Italo Balbo successfully to organize *squadristi* with truncheons and castor oil to frighten the Socialists from their positions of influence in the towns and countryside. This wave of violence got underway in the late summer of 1920 and achieved its goal in remarkably short order. Fascism took on an entirely new aspect as it branched out from its urban birthplace, Milan (where it seemed destined to extinction by 1920), to gain strongholds in the farming areas of the lower Po valley, Venezia Giulia, Tuscany, and elsewhere. Henceforth, Fascism was to be allied to right-wing groups and eventually the monarchy and the Church. A narrower discussion of the situation in Ferrara is Alessandro Roveri, *Le origini del fascismo a Ferrara, 1918-1921* (Milan, 1974).

Another localized study of the Po valley has been undertaken by Francis J. Demers, *Le origini del fascismo a Cremona* (Bari, 1979). Cremona's bellicose *ras* (Fascist boss), who played a major role in launching the "second wave" that resulted in the totalitarian state in 1925-26, is the subject of a spotty biography by Harry Fornari, *Mussolini's Gadfly: Roberto Farinacci* (Nashville, 1971). Mario Vaini has published *Le origini del fascismo a Mantova* (Rome, 1961). Anthony L. Cardoza sheds light on "The Agrarian Elites and the Origins of Italian Fascism: The Province of Bologna, 1901-1922" (unpublished doctoral thesis, Princeton University, 1976). Lawrence L. Squeri has written "Politics in Parma, 1900-1925: The Rise of Fascism" (unpublished doctoral thesis, University of Pennsylvania, 1976). A. A. Kelikian has completed a study, "From Liberalism to Corporatism: Brescia, 1915-1926" (unpublished doctoral thesis. Oxford University, 1978).

The region of Venezia Giulia, adjacent to Yugoslavia, is discussed in Elio Apih, *Italia, fascismo e antifascismo nella Venezia Giulia (1918-1943)* (Bari, 1966), while Simona Colarizi describes the postwar situation in the heel of the Italian boot in *Dopoguerra e fascismo in Puglia (1919-1926)* (Bari, 1971). Elsewhere in the South it took longer for the Fascists to establish a strong foothold. Both Fascism and the Sardinian autonomy movement are examined in Salvatore Sechi, *Dopoguerra e fascismo in Sardegna: Il movimento autonomistico nella crisi dello Stato liberale (1918-1926)* (Turin, 1969). Two volumes of papers presented at a symposium sponsored by the provincial government of Florence give an excellent account of Tuscany's experiences: *La Toscana nel regime fascista (1922-1939)* (Florence, 1971). These can be supplemented by Roberto Cantagalli, *Storia del fascismo fiorentino, 1919-1925* (Florence, 1972), and Marco Palla, *Firenze nel regime fascista (1929-1934)* (Florence, 1978).

Fascist Social and Economic Policies

The classic work in English on social and economic policies was *Mussolini's Italy* (New York, 1935; reissued,

1965), by the political scientist Herman Finer. Writing during the last period of the Fascist era, he was able to evaluate the regime in its mature form. Finer's judgment, rendered calmly and dispassionately, was negative. A year later Gaetano Salvemini published a much more polemical, hard-hitting book, *Under the Axe of Fascism* (New York, 1936), which described Mussolini's Italy as a conglomerate oligarchy made up of four groups: army chiefs, high civil servants, big businessmen, and party leaders. The interlocking and mutually reinforcing interests of these four groups gave the regime its internal coherence and stability. "In this oligarchy the big capitalists" were "far from exercising an uncontested sway ... If the capitalists stopped playing the policies of the Party, the Party could easily steer to the left. Thus, although the employers" were "protected," they were "intimidated at the same time." (pp. 383-85).

In 1938 the economist Carl T. Schmidt set forth a withering analysis of Fascism's agrarian policies in *The Plough and the Sword: Labor, Land and Property in Fascist Italy* (New York). He has also written *The Corporate State in Action: Italy under Fascism* (New York, 1939). Still another excellent study of that vintage is William G. Welk, *Fascist Economic Policy: An Analysis of Italy's Economic Experiment* (Cambridge, Mass., 1938). In French there were also two highly critical books by Louis Rosenstock-Franck, *L'économie corporative fasciste en doctrine et en fait*, 2 vols. (Paris, 1934), and *Les étapes de l'économie fasciste italienne* (Paris, 1939).

Writing from the vantage of a quarter century after the fall of Fascism, Roland Sarti, a nuanced Marxist historian, has given us a penetrating and succinct monograph, *Fascism and the Industrial Leadership in Italy, 1919-1940: A Study in the Expansion of Private Power under Fascism* (Berkeley, 1971). Making use of new documentation, he confirms the findings of Rosenstock-Franck, Schmidt, and others. Sarti stresses that during the Fascist regime the industrialists remained largely self-organized in the Confindustria, whereas the emasculated labor organizations had their leaders selected for them by the Fascist party, which always kept them on short leash. The industrialists were delighted to be rid of the powerful Socialist and Catholic unions and to see the Fascist syndicates largely impotent. Sarti's article, "Fascist Modernization in Italy: Traditional or Revolutionary?" *American Historical Review* 75 (Apr. 1970): 1029-45, is an insightful inquiry into that controversial topic, as is Alberto

Aquarone, "Aspirazioni technocratiche del primo fascismo," *Nord e Sud* 11 (Apr. 1964): 109–28. Sarti has also edited an anthology, *The Ax Within: Italian Fascism in Action* (New York, 1974). It includes a number of articles by present-day Italian specialists in economic and social history that he has translated.

Less satisfactory is a recent book by the political scientist A. James Gregor, *Italian Fascism and Developmental Dictatorship* (Princeton, 1979). Whereas most writers have tended to view Italian Fascism as a phenomenon unique to the developmental experience of Europe, Gregor argues otherwise. According to him, Italian Fascism is far from being specifically European; it is simply one variant of a class of "developmental ideologies" that trace their origins to Marxist thinking. This is an argument that he had developed earlier in *The Ideology of Fascism: The Rationale of Totalitarianism* (New York, 1969). Gregor links Fascism to Bolshevik Russia, Castro's Cuba, and a number of Third World movements. He contends that all of them sought to modernize and industrialize their respective national communities and created analogous strategies and institutions to do so. Several critics have expressed doubt as to the accuracy of Gregor's thesis and to the usefulness of trying to equate Fascism with such diverse regimes. Moreover, there is skepticism that Mussolini's chief interest was really economic modernization.

A study by Gino Germani, *Authoritarianism, Fascism, and National Populism* (New Brunswick, N.J., 1978), fits the fascist experience into the broad category "modern authoritarianism," one of whose forms is "totalitarianism." Germani finds the fascist phenomenon relative not only to Mussolini's Italy but to Hitler's Germany and several Latin American countries.

Charles S. Maier is the author of a sophisticated comparative study, *Recasting Bourgeois Europe: Stabilization in France, Germany, and Italy in the Decade after World War I* (Princeton, 1975). Maier contends that all three of these countries were moving from classical parliamentarism toward "corporatist" patterns of representation by interest groups. His conclusion is that this system of stability, despite its interruption by the Great Depression, Nazism, and World War II, anticipated political solutions achieved after 1945.

For corporativism's attraction among circles outside Italy, one may turn to Alastair Hamilton, *The Appeal of Fascism* (London, 1971), and to John P. Diggins, *Mussolini and Fascism: The View from*

America (Princeton, 1972). A specialist in American intellectual history, Diggins has made a detailed investigation of the attitudes of a number of American political, economic, religious, and intellectual groups toward the Blackshirt dictatorship during the 1920s and 1930s when it enjoyed considerable popularity in the United States. Mussolini's antibolshevism, his accommodation with the Church, and his corporativist experiments all contributed to his popularity in these circles. Jens Petersen has discussed the "view from Weimar Germany" in an article, "Il fascismo visto dalla Repubblica di Weimar," *Storia contemporanea* 9 (June 1978): 497-529. A study of English public opinion that is restricted to the first half of the 1920s, and thus before the era of corporativism, is Aldo Berselli, *L'opinione pubblica inglese e l'avvento del fascismo* (Milan, 1971).

Among the major studies of the relationship of Fascism to big business are Ernesto Rossi, *Padroni del vapore e fascismo* (Bari, 1966), written with passion by a radical democrat who spent several years in Fascist prisons; Piero Melograni's more restrained analysis, *Gli industriali e Mussolini: Rapporti tra Confindustria e fascismo dal 1919 al 1929* (Milan, 1972); and the Socialist Valerio Castronovo's recent biography of the elder *Giovanni Agnelli* (Turin, 1971), who founded Fiat in Turin in 1899 and dominated it until his death in 1945. Bruno Caizzi has written a biography of *Camillo e Adriano Olivetti* (Turin, 1962), whose typewriter and office machines factory at Ivrea achieved international fame. Finally, one may note a collection of essays by Marxist historians: *Fascismo e capitalismo,* ed. Nicola Tranfaglia (Milan, 1976).

The question of whether Fascist Italy was truly "totalitarian" has been taken up in two important studies. Arguing in favor of this interpretation is *The Italian Fascist Party in Power: A Study in Totalitarian Rule* (Minneapolis, 1959), by an American political scientist, Dante L. Germino, who tends to follow Carl J. Friedrich's paradigm of totalitarianism. An Italian political scientist, Alberto Aquarone, on the other hand, believes that the regime fell short of being truly totalitarian despite the fact that it employed this term. He argues that the Fascist party was steadily absorbed by the State, rather than vice versa. Aquarone's fat book, *L'organizzazione dello Stato totalitario* (Turin, 1965), is buttressed by many relevant documents.

An anthology, *Fascismo e societa italiana,* ed. Guido Quazza (Turin,

1973), contains a number of important essays on the Fascist economy, the army, the judiciary, the Church, and culture. These Italian authors generally stress the theme of "continuity," i.e., that Fascism did not represent an abrupt break with what preceded and what followed, a thesis that is particularly popular among leftists.

Broader but somewhat uneven in its coverage is Edward R. Tannenbaum, *The Fascist Experience: Italian Society and Culture, 1922-1945* (New York, 1972). It is especially helpful in illustrating Fascist policies in the fields of education, popular culture, literature, and the arts. Alexander J. De Grand has written an excellent book, *Bottai e la cultura fascista* (Rome, 1978), on the Fascist hierarch, Giuseppe Bottai, who edited the review, *Critica fascista,* served as minister of education from 1936 to 1943, and drew up the School Charter of 1939 that proposed to bring work experience into the educational process. In July 1943 Bottai was one of the hierarchs who plotted the coup d'état against the Duce. His own memoirs, *Vent'anni e un giorno (24 luglio 1943)* (Milan, 1949), are informative. A French specialist on Fascist Italy, Michel Ostenc, has recently published a significant study, *L'éducation en Italie pendant le fascisme* (Paris, 1980).

By the late 1930s cynicism was setting in among many members of the "generation of the Littoriali," including those students who had enrolled in the Gioventù Universitaria Fascista (GUF). They had come to sense that the corporative state was a sham, that the party was being dominated by Achille Starace, its boorish secretary (1932-39), and that Mussolini was offering them only a series of wars and closer ties to Hitler's Germany. This disillusionment is revealed in Ruggero Zangrandi, *Il lungo viaggio attraverso il fascismo* (Milan, 1962). It is also depicted in Luigi Preti's documentary novel of the years 1936-1945, *Giovinezza! Giovinezza!* (Milan, 1963; English trans., *Through the Fascist Fire* [London, 1968]). Tannenbaum touches upon it in chapters 6 and 10 of his book, as does Michael A. Ledeen in his article, "Italian Fascism and Youth," *Journal of Contemporary History* 4 (July 1969): 137-54. Tracy H. Koon, "Believe, Obey, Fight: Political Socialization of Youth in Fascist Italy, 1922-1943" (unpublished doctoral thesis, Stanford University, 1977), is also informative. The war years 1940-43 proved the final disillusionment for those young Fascist idealists who believed in what De Felice called "fascismo-movimento." Philip V. Cannistraro's monograph, *La fabbrica del consenso: Fascismo e mass media* (Bari, 1975), is a study of the ways in which the Ministry of Popular Culture, which was created in 1933, used the mass media to fabricate the consensus that Fascism claimed to enjoy among the populace.

Feminism got little support from the Blackshirts. A pioneering monograph on the emergence of feminism in the Italian political parties from 1919 until the imposition of the dictatorship has been written by Franca Pieroni Bortolotti, *Feminismo e partiti politici in Italia, 1919-1926* (Rome, 1978).

Church and State in Fascist Italy

From the unification of Italy in 1870 until 1929 there was no formal recognition of the Kingdom by the Holy See. Mussolini's negotiation of the Lateran pacts (treaty, concordat, and financial agreement) with the Vatican on February 11, 1929, proved to be the most lasting accomplishment of the dictatorship. It resulted in mutual diplomatic recognition, the proclaiming of Roman Catholicism as the official religion, and called upon the State to enforce canon law with respect to the marriage sacrament. As a result, Italy became the most clerical state in Europe. The major work in English on this and other aspects of Italian relations with the Holy See is *Church and State in Fascist Italy* (London, 1941; reprinted, New York, 1970, with new preface), by an Irish liberal Catholic scholar, Daniel A. Binchy. Generally balanced in his assessments of papal policy, he does not hesitate to be critical whenever such criticism is required. Binchy can be taken to task, however, for exaggerating the resistance of the Vatican officials to Fascism and underestimating that of the lower clergy.

Published soon after World War II and without knowledge of Binchy's book was a major Italian historical study undertaken by a liberal Catholic specialist, Arturo Carlo Jemolo, *Chiesa e Stato negli ultimi cento anni* (Turin, 1949; rev. ed., 1963). An abridged version is available in English: *Church and State in Italy, 1850-1950* (Oxford, 1960). Jemolo's student, Francesco Margiotta Broglio, has written *Italia e Santa Sede dalla grande guerra alla conciliazione* (Bari, 1966). A scholarly study of the 1924-29 period is Sandro Rogari, *Santa Sede e fascismo: Dall'Aventino ai Patti Lateranensi* (Bologna, 1977).

A recent monograph by Philip V. Cannistraro and Gianfausto Rosoli, *Emigrazione, Chiesa, e fascismo: Lo scioglimento dell'Opera Bonomelli (1922-28)* (Rome, 1979), explores the rivalry between

Mussolini's regime and the Church in looking after the interests of Italian emigrants in Western Europe. The Opera Bonomelli had been founded at the turn of the century by Bishop Bonomelli of Cremona, who believed that the Church should provide assistance to Italian emigrants. When Mussolini came to power he manipulated subsidies and personnel changes within the Opera Bonomelli so as to bring it increasingly under Fascist control. The Vatican decided to dissolve the organization in 1928 in order to facilitate the negotiations then underway for the Lateran pacts.

An American historian, Richard A. Webster, has written a valuable, though somewhat choppy study of the relations of Mussolini's regime with the Italian Popolare party, the Catholic Action movement of the laity, and the clandestine activities of Catholics during the dictatorship and Armed Resistance: *The Cross and the Fasces: Christian Democracy and Fascism in Italy* (Stanford, 1960). Supplementing this is a recent book by an Australian, John N. Molony, *The Emergence of Political Catholicism in Italy: Partito Popolare 1919-1926* (London, 1977), which focuses primarily on the founder of that party, the Sicilian priest, Luigi Sturzo.

The standard biography of this remarkable figure who was forced into exile in 1924 and did not return until after the war is *Luigi Sturzo (1871-1959)* (Turin, 1977), by Gabriele De Rosa, who was in close touch with him during the final years and who helped to organize his archives. De Rosa has also written *Storia del Partito popolare* (Bari, 1958) and *Storia politica dell'Azione cattolica in Italia,* 2 vols. (Bari, 1953-54). Sturzo's collected works, *Opera omnia,* 12 vols. (Bologna, 1962 ff.), have been supplemented by his previously unpublished writings, *Scritti inediti,* 3 vols., ed. Gabriele De Rosa (Rome, 1974-76).

When Sturzo was compelled to leave Italy, Alcide De Gasperi, a native of the Trentino, became the principal leader of the Popolare party until its dissolution two years later. He spent the years of the dictatorship partly in prison but mostly working inconspicuously in the Vatican libraries. In 1943 he emerged as head of the powerful new Democrazia Cristiana (Christian Democratic party). Elisa Carrillo has chronicled his activities during those years: *Alcide De Gasperi: The Long Apprenticeship* (Notre Dame, 1965). His articles of that era have been collected in *I cattolici dall'opposizione al governo* (Bari, 1955).

Anthony Rhodes, *The Vatican in the Age of the Dictators, 1922-1945* (London, 1973), is a rather uncritical survey of the Vatican's relationship to the regimes of Mussolini and Hitler. The author strongly defends Pius XII's behavior during World War II. Charles F. Delzell, ed., *The Papacy and Totalitarianism Between the Two World Wars* (New York, 1974), is a problem-book that seeks to set forth conflicting views on this highly controversial subject. His article, "Pius XII, Italy, and the Outbreak of War," *Journal of Contemporary History* 2 (Oct. 1967): 137-62, deals with the period September 1939-June 1940 and is based on the recently published documents of the Holy See: Secrétairerie d'État de Sa Sainteté, *Actes et documents du Saint Siège relatifs à la seconde guerre mondiale* (Vatican City, 1965 ff.), of which an English translation is being prepared by Gerard Noel for Herder Publications, London, and Corpus Books, Washington and Cleveland. *Vatican Diplomacy and the Jews during the Holocaust, 1939-1943* (New York, 1980), by John F. Morley, a Roman Catholic priest in Newark, is a sharp criticism of what he feels was the Vatican's muted response to this crisis, about which it had considerable information.

Death in Rome (New York, 1967), by the American journalist, Robert Katz, is an hour-by-hour account of the activities of various groups in German-occupied Rome in March 1944 which led to the slaying of 33 German soldiers on the street by young Italian partisans. The Nazis ordered a retaliation at a ratio of more than ten to one. Thus, 335 Italians (most of them Jews) were taken from the prisons to the Ardeatine Caves, where they were shot. Katz is highly critical of the alleged reluctance of the Vatican to take a more vigorous stance against the Nazi measures.

The most thorough study of the problem of the Jews under Italian Fascism is a recent long book by the Israeli historian Meir Michaelis, *Mussolini and the Jews: German-Italian Relations and the Jewish Question in Italy, 1922-1945* (Oxford, 1978). Michaelis makes clear that the anti-Semitic legislation in Italy of 1938, though facilitated by the example of the Nazis and pleasing to them, was neither demanded nor imposed by Hitler. The author takes into consideration Mussolini's difficulties vis-à-vis the Germans but at the same time he shows the Duce's lack of moral principles. He also illuminates the latent anti-Semitism that existed in Italy. Michaelis corrects and supplements Renzo De Felice's pioneering study, *Storia degli ebrei italiani sotto il fascismo* (Turin, 1961). Gene Bernardini's article, "Origins and Development of Racial Anti-Semitism in Fascist Italy," *Journal of Modern History* 49 (Sept. 1977): 431-53, is also a worthy contribution. It points up both the influence of the Ethiopian War and Mussolini's efforts to distinguish between Italian racism and German racism. The former was supposed to be political, not biological. For a discussion of the colonial background to Fascist racism, one can turn to two books by Luigi Preti, *I miti dell'impero e della razza nell'Italia degli anni '30* (Rome, 1965), and *Impero fascista, africani ed ebrei* (Milan, 1968). De Felice has published recently a book on the Jews in Italian Libya, *Ebrei in un paese arabo* (Bologna, 1978). It is a valuable complement to his previous work on the Jews in Fascist Italy.

Comparative Studies of Fascism

Renzo De Felice was the first postwar Italian scholar to undertake a systematic study of "generic" or "universal" fascism (spelled with a small "f") and to analyze the various interpretations of it. In 1969 he published a manual surveying this literature, as well as a companion anthology of texts: *Interpretazioni del fascismo* (Bari, 1969); and *Il fascismo: Le interpretazioni dei contemporanei e degli storici* (Bari, 1970). The former has recently appeared in English as *Interpretations of Fascism* (Cambridge, Mass., 1977). De Felice's analysis was stimulated by Ernst Nolte's important but often abstruse comparative study, *Three Faces of Fascism: Action Française, Italian Fascism, National Socialism* (New York, 1966),[17] and by Eugen Weber's compact discussion, *Varieties of Fascism: Doctrines of Revolution in the 20th Century* (New York, 1964).

De Felice divides his *Interpretations of Fascism* into two sections. In the first, he surveys fascism as a generic European phenomenon and discusses much of the literature on the subject. In Part Two he turns to Italian Fascism, concentrating here on the writings of Italian scholars and politicians. In his judgment, there have been three "classic" interpretations: (1) the thesis that fascism was an interlude, a kind of "moral sickness" that afflicted not just Italy but other parts of Europe as well—a contention that had the support of Benedetto Croce; (2) the radical thesis of Giustino Fortunato, Piero

---

[17]The original German edition was entitled *Der Faschismus in seiner Epoche* (Munich, 1963). Nolte has also edited *Theorien über den Faschismus* (Cologne, 1970).

Gobetti, and others that fascism was simply a "revelation" of historical tendencies deeply ingrained in certain countries like Italy and Germany; and (3) the Marxist argument—which was the earliest to be propounded—that fascism was an antiproletarian reaction that was a product of capitalist society in its highest stage regardless of country. In other sections De Felice takes up the Catholic interpretation, the "totalitarian" school of analysis, and Nolte's "metapolitical" approach to the problem. Lastly, he surveys the interpretations offered by social scientists, commenting especially on the psychosocial, sociological, and socioeconomic explanations that have been suggested.

Part Two, which deals with Italian interpretations of Italian Fascism, touches upon the explanations set forth prior to the assassination of Matteotti in 1924—commenting especially on Luigi Salvatorelli's pioneering analysis in 1923 which emphasized the petty bourgeois nature of Fascism, and on the Fascists' own rationale of their new "ism." De Felice then considers the interpretations that were published during the years of the dictatorship—both those written at home by Fascists and those written abroad by exiles. Another chapter takes up the post-Liberation debate, while the final section sets forth his own conclusions regarding the social bases of Fascism in Italy and his conviction that fascism must be viewed as a peculiarly European phenomenon of the period bracketed by two World Wars.

In the years since writing *Interpretations of Fascism* in 1969, De Felice has minimized the similarities between Mussolini's Fascism and Hitler's National Socialism, emphasizing instead the differences. Although he concedes that certain factions within Italian Fascism saw eye to eye with National Socialism, he now insists that the bulk of Italian Fascism was born on the Left and stood in the optimistic political tradition of Rousseau and of Robespierre's current of the "general will" and "totalitarian democracy." Most Italian Fascists had faith in the possibility of creating a "new Fascist man," he argues, whereas the Nazis sought from the outset to restore old values.

De Felice's insistence upon the "substantial" differences between German Nazism and most of Italian Fascism has met with skepticism in some quarters. The majority of historians are quite ready, of course, to concede that anti-Semitism was far more prevalent in

National Socialism than in Italian Fascism, and also that Hitler was able to impose far more effective "totalitarian" control over the Germans than Mussolini ever could over the Italians. But these differences probably do not overshadow the essential affinity of the two movements and regimes, a similarity that was demonstrated not only in their common antiliberalism, anti-Marxism, antimaterialism, and antiplutocracy propaganda but also by the fact that they came together ideologically in the Axis and the Pact of Steel, and by the fact that they fought on the same side in the Spanish Civil War and in World War II from 1940 to 1943 (and in northern Italy for two more years). As De Felice himself conceded this point in his earlier writings, it is somewhat surprising that he has now shifted his posture and looks upon Mussolini's attack on France as simply an opportunistic move undertaken by a vacillating Duce who expected a quick victory.

In addition to the comparative studies mentioned above, one should call attention to several others. *Fascism: Comparison and Definition* (Madison, 1980), by Stanley G. Payne, a specialist on Spain, is up-to-date and succinct. Walter C. Laqueur, ed., *Fascism: A Reader's Guide* (Berkeley, 1976), brings together a useful collection of analytical and historiographical essays by the political sociologist Juan J. Linz, the historian Adrian Lyttelton, and specialists from several countries. They deal with fascism in Italy, Germany, and other parts of Europe and Latin America. *Interpretations of Fascism* (Morristown, N.J., 1974), by the social scientist A. James Gregor, discusses somewhat sardonically the various schools of thought that see fascism as, respectively, a consequence of class struggle, of moral crisis, of psychological disabilities, and of the rise of the "amorphous masses." Gregor finds all of these interpretations unsatisfactory. He prefers to look for the answers under the formulae of fascism as a stage of modernization and a form of totalitarianism. Alan Cassels, in *Fascism* (New York, 1975), sees a dichotomy between the "forward-looking" corporativist ideology of Italian Fascism and the "backward-looking" *völkisch* racism which informed the entire German National Socialist experience. He ascribes this to the relative stages of modernization reached by Italy in 1922 and Germany in 1933. He suggests a "Janus-faced" theory of fascism that will accommodate both the Italian and German varieties. Charles F. Delzell, ed., *Mediterranean Fascism, 1919–1945,* which has already been cited, provides a comparative documentary history of Fascism in Italy and of the semifascistic movements in Spain and Portugal. Stuart J. Woolf, ed., *European Fascism* (New York, 1968), brings together papers on this murky subject that were presented at an international symposium held at the University of Reading. Hans Rogger and Eugen Weber have edited a volume of essays, *The European Right: A Historical Profile* (Berkeley, 1965), that examines several countries, while F. L. Carsten uses a comparative approach in *The Rise of Fascism* (Berkeley, 1967). Nicos Poulantzas's *Fascism and Dictatorship* (London, 1974), though rejecting the narrow "economism" of the Stalinist era that depicted fascism as the tool of monopoly capitalism, is nonetheless still hedged in by *a priori* assumptions. A number of papers pertaining to Italy were among those presented at an international symposium in 1974 in Norway on the theme, *Who Were the Fascists? Social Roots of European Fascism* (Bergen, Oslo, Tromso, 1980), ed. Stein Ugelvik Larsen and others.

The diversity of informed opinion regarding the possibility of "generic" fascism is dazzling—so much so that Gilbert Allardyce, in a provocative essay, "What Fascism is Not: Thoughts on the Deflation of a Concept," *American Historical Review* 84 (Apr. 1979): 367–98, expresses doubts whether there really is a "paradigmatic" or "universal" fascism. Finally, to supplement the above discussions, mention should be made of a review-article by Charles S. Maier, "Some Recent Studies of Fascism," *Journal of Modern History* 48 (Sept. 1976): 506–21.

Fascist Foreign Policy

Since the overthrow of Fascism the Italian Ministry of Foreign Affairs has been editing and publishing one hundred volumes of *I Documenti diplomatici italiani* (Rome, 1952 ff.), covering the period 1861 to 1943 in nine series. The project is now one-third complete. Access to this kind of archival material is making possible the rewriting of much of the history of Italian foreign policy. Thus, the prewar account by Maxwell H. H. Macartney and Paul Cremona, *Italy's Foreign and Colonial Policy 1914–1937* (London, 1938), has been superseded by a number of studies, the broadest of which is the outline history by Cedric J. Lowe and F. Marzari, *Italian Foreign Policy, 1870–1940* (London, 1975). For the period up to 1925, Christopher Seton-Watson's book, already mentioned, is good.

Alan Cassells of McMaster University in Canada is now preparing a bibliographical handbook of Italian foreign policy between 1918 and 1945. He has already published *Mussolini's Early Diplomacy* (Princeton, 1970), a well-documented and balanced study of the years 1922-27, while for the preceding period we have Giorgio Rumi, *Alle origini della politica estera fascista, 1918-1923* (Bari, 1968). In Italian there is Giampiero Carocci, *La politica estera dell'Italia fascista (1925-1928)* (Bari, 1969). Ennio Di Nolfo, *Mussolini e la politica estera italiana, 1919-1933* (Padua, 1960), is dated, as he did not make use of German sources. All of these studies now supersede Gaetano Salvemini's acerbic account, *Mussolini diplomatico, 1922-1932* (rev. ed., Bari, 1952). James Barros, a political scientist, has written an exhaustive study of the 1923 dispute between Italy and Greece, the first major issue to involve a Great Power that the League had to confront: *The Corfu Incident of 1923: Mussolini and the League of Nations* (Princeton, 1965).

The initial decade of Fascist diplomacy has also been examined by H. Stuart Hughes in a chapter in Felix Gilbert and Gordon A. Craig, eds., *The Diplomats, 1919-1939* (Princeton, 1953), but it is now largely outdated. In this same collection Gilbert wrote a discerning essay on Mussolini's son-in-law and foreign minister, "Ciano and his Ambassadors." The fascinating diaries of Ciano, available in English, provide a first-hand account of the development of the Duce's policies but they cannot always be taken at face value: Count Galeazzo Ciano, *The Ciano Diaries, 1939-1943,* ed. Hugh Gibson (Garden City, N.Y., 1945), and *Ciano's Diplomatic Papers,* ed. Malcolm Muggeridge (London, 1948). Major biographies of the Duce's protégé include Duilio Susmel, *Vita sbagliata di Galeazzo Ciano* (Milan, 1962), and Giordano Bruno Guerri, *Galeazzo Ciano: Una vita, 1903-1944* (Milan, 1979). Marcia F. Lavine, author of "Count Galeazzo Ciano: Foreign Affairs and Policy Determination in Fascist Italy, January 1939-June 1940" (unpublished doctoral thesis, Vanderbilt University, 1977), has written a profile of Ciano in Ferdinando Cordova, ed., *Uomini e volti del fascismo,* cited previously.

Italy's dictatorship devoted considerable attention to promoting pro-Fascist activities in other countries. Michael A. Ledeen's *Universal Fascism: The Theory and Practice of the Fascist International, 1928-1936* (New York, 1972) is an interesting monograph that explores the little-known and abortive efforts of certain Italian Fascists to establish an international Fascist organization under their aegis that would popularize "corporative state" ideas abroad. Their effort failed because of strong national differences and especially because of the stronger influence exerted by Hitler's National Socialists after 1933. With respect to Fascist activities in the United States, Gaetano Salvemini prepared a confidential exposé for American officials in World War II. It has recently been published: *Italian Fascist Activities in the United States,* ed. Philip V. Cannistraro (New York, 1977).

Fascist Italy's discriminatory treatment of its Germanic and Slavic minorities in the frontier provinces of the Alto Adige (South Tyrol) and Venezia Giulia is discussed systematically by Dennison I. Rusinow in *Italy's Austrian Heritage, 1919-1946* (New York, 1969).

The background and course of the conflict between Italy and Haile Selassie's Ethiopia has, of course, aroused much interest among historians and journalists. Salvemini's *Prelude to World War II* (London, 1953), based on newspaper sources, was a strong indictment of British as well as of Italian policies in the mid-1930s. It has been superseded by painstakingly detailed studies undertaken by the American, George W. Baer, in *The Coming of the Italian-Ethiopian War* (Cambridge, Mass., 1967) and its sequel, *Test Case: Italy, Ethiopia, and the League of Nations* (Stanford, 1976), which give full attention to the international ramifications of the crisis; and also by the British scholar, Esmonde M. Robertson, *Mussolini as Empire-Builder: Europe and Africa 1932-36* (London, 1977). Writing with a popular audience in mind, A. J. Barker highlights the military aspects in *The Civilizing Mission: A History of the Italo-Ethiopian War* (New York, 1968), as does Thomas M. Coffey in *Lion By the Tail* (New York, 1974). James Dugan and Laurence Lafore, in their book *Days of Emperor and Clown: The Italo-Ethiopian War, 1935-1936* (New York, 1974), deal more inclusively with the military, diplomatic, political, and social dimensions of the conflict. A first-rate Italian study of the preparations for this war has been published by Giorgio Rochat, *Militari e politici nella preparazione della campagna d'Etiopia: Studio e documenti, 1932-1936* (Milan, 1971). Samuel K. B. Asante, *Pan-African Protest: West Africa and the Italo-Ethiopian Crisis, 1934-1941* (London, 1978), is written by a political scientist at the University of Ghana. He discusses the effect of the conflict on British colonies in West Africa and thus offers a new perspective on the war.

Mussolini's Roman Empire (New York, 1976), by Denis Mack Smith, is a wide-ranging, hard-hitting book that centers on the foreign policy of the 1930s. Readers will be amused by the author's collection of colorful quotations that in retrospect reveal Mussolini to have been largely a poseur, but the overall quality of this book falls short of Mack Smith's previous ones. John F. Coverdale has given us a satisfactory account of *Italian Intervention in the Spanish Civil War* (Princeton, 1975), but he does a better job describing the military actions than in explaining the motivations for Italian intervention and the repercussions at home.

It was Italian intervention in the Spanish conflict that finally threw Mussolini into Hitler's arms. The perception of this war as a polarized struggle between a fascist Right and communist Left appealed to him greatly. The Rome-Berlin Axis, which emerged in the autumn of 1936, was first analyzed by Elizabeth Wiskemann in *The Rome-Berlin Axis: A History of the Relations Between Hitler and Mussolini* (London, 1949). Now somewhat dated, her book must be supplemented by D. C. Watt's article, "The Rome-Berlin Axis, 1936-40: Myth and Reality," *Review of Politics* 22 (1960): 519-43, and Jens Petersen's book, *Hitler-Mussolini: Die Entstehung der Achse Berlin-Rom 1933-1936* (Tübingen, 1973). For the ensuing military alliance of May 1939 with Nazi Germany, one should consult D. C. Watt's article, "An Earlier Model for the Pact of Steel: The Draft Treaties Exchanged between Germany and Italy during Hitler's Visit to Rome in May 1938," *International Affairs* 33 (1957): 185-97, and Mario Toscano's book, *The Origins of the Pact of Steel* (Baltimore, 1967). On earlier Fascist and Nazi links one must read K.-P. Hoepke, *Die Deutsche Rechte und der italienische Faschismus* (Düsseldorf, 1968). Toscano, who enjoyed access to the archives of the Italian Ministry of Foreign Affairs, has also published a collection of trenchant essays on Italian diplomacy in this period: *Designs in Diplomacy* (Baltimore, 1970).

When Hitler's Germany invaded Poland in September 1939, thereby unleashing World War II, Mussolini quickly proclaimed that Italy would remain "non-belligerent." He brought Italy into the war on June 10, 1940, when Hitler's blitzkrieg in the West had forced France to her knees. Thereafter, the Duce fought what he termed a "parallel war" alongside Germany against Britain, the Soviet Union, and later the United States. One of the best accounts of the vacillating steps taken by Italy between the Munich Conference of 1938 and entry into the world conflict is Ferdinand Siebert, *Italiens Weg in den Zweiten Weltkrieg* (Frankfurt-am-Main/Bonn, 1962). He made use of published Italian, German, and British diplomatic documents. MacGregor Knox, *Mussolini Unleashed, 1939-1941: Politics and Strategy in Fascist Italy's Last War* (New York, 1980), is a valuable contribution to scholarship. Among the numerous books on Fascist Italy's role in World War II, particular mention should be made of these fairly recent ones: Josef Schröder's meticulous bibliographical guide, *Italien im Zweiten Weltkrieg: Eine Bibliographie* (Munich, 1978); Emilio Faldella, *L'Italia e la seconda guerra mondiale* (Bologna, 1960); Giorgio Bocca, *Storia d'Italia nella guerra fascista 1940-1943* (Bari, 1969); Lucio Ceva, *La condotta italiana della guerra: Cavallero e il comando supremo 1941/42* (Milan, 1974); and *Generali, servizi segreti e fascismo* (Milan, 1978), a study by Carlo De Risio, a former member of Italy's secret military intelligence (SIM). Mussolini's bungled invasion of Greece in October 1940 has been described by an Italian participant, Mario Cervi, *The Hollow Legions: Mussolini's Blunders in Greece, 1940-1941* (London, 1972).

The Anti-Fascist Opposition

Thus far, the only book to cover the entire spectrum of anti-Fascist activities from the assassination of the democratic socialist leader Giacomo Matteotti[18] in June 1924 until the final liberation of the North in April 1945 is Charles F. Delzell's lengthy book, *Mussolini's Enemies: The Italian Anti-Fascist Resistance* (Princeton, 1961; rev. ed., New York, 1973). The first half discusses both the "quiet" wing of anti-Fascism, which was made up especially of Catholics and of Liberals like Benedetto Croce who remained at home during the dictatorship, and the more "activist" wing that carried out clandestine opposition both in Italy and abroad until 1943. The latter group included the Communists, Socialists, and Giustizia e Libertà. The last half of the book covers the coup d'état of July 5, 1943, the emergence of open anti-Fascism in the liberated South, and the upsurge of Armed Resistance in the German-occupied North after September 8, 1943. Delzell's review-article, "The Italian Anti-Fascist Resistance in Retrospect: Three Decades

---

[18] A sympathetic biography, *Matteotti: Una vita per il socialismo* (Milan, 1974), has been written by Antonio G. Casanova. Among the recent studies of the assassination and ensuing "Aventine" crisis are Ariane Landuyt, *Le sinistre e l'Aventino* (Milan, 1973), and Giovanni Rossini, *Il delitto Matteotti tra il Viminale e l'Aventino* (Bologna, 1966).

of Historiography," *Journal of Modern History* 47 (Mar. 1975): 66–96, surveys this burgeoning literature.

Among the large numbers of working-class Italian emigrants in France and other countries during the years of the dictatorship were some ten thousand political refugees. They included prominent figures from the entire political spectrum. The high point of their struggle coincided with the Spanish Civil War. The classic work in Italian on the activities of these émigrés is *Storia dei fuorusciti* (Bari, 1953), by Aldo Garosci, who was a militant in Giustizia e Libertà, the liberal-socialist movement founded in 1929 by the Florentine Jew and former student of Salvemini, Carlo Rosselli. It functioned in France and covertly in Italy until Carlo and his brother Nello were assassinated by Fascist agents in Normandy in 1937. Soon after the overthrow of the dictatorship, Garosci published a two-volume *Vita di Carlo Rosselli* (Rome, 1945). These studies have now been supplemented by important papers presented by Garosci, Leo Valiani, Gaetano Arfè, Roberto Vivarelli, and others at a symposium held in Florence in June 1977 under Carlo Francovich's leadership: *"Giustizia e Libertà" nella lotta antifascista e nella storia d'Italia: Attualità dei fratelli Rosselli a quaranta anni dal loro sacrificio* (Florence, 1978). Frank Rosengarten has recently written a biography of one of Giustizia e Libertà's principal leaders, *Silvio Trentin dall'interventismo alla resistenza* (Milan, 1980). He has also published a monograph that seeks to analyze the role of *The Italian Anti-Fascist Press, 1919–1945: From the Legal Opposition Press to the Underground Newspapers of World War II* (Cleveland, 1968). Paolo Alatri, a Communist, has edited a collection of newspaper articles and other documents: *L'antifascismo italiano*, 2 vols., (3rd ed., Rome, 1973). The major Communist study of that party's role in the underground is Paolo Spriano's five-volume *Storia del Partito comunista italiano* (Turin, 1967–75), which will be discussed in a later section.

Coup d'État, July 25, 1943

Italy's repeated military setbacks in the war, climaxed by the successful Allied invasion of Sicily on July 10, 1943, precipitated the coup d'état on July 25 which overthrew Mussolini's regime. The overlapping conspiracies involved certain high army officials, the aged king, and dissident hierarchs (Grandi, Bottai, Ciano, etc.) in the Fascist Grand Council. The most detailed account is Gianfranco Bianchi, *25 luglio: Crollo di un regime* (Milan,

1964). Mussolini's own memoirs have appeared in two editions in English: *The Fall of Mussolini,* ed. Max Ascoli (New York, 1948), and *Memoirs, 1942-1943,* ed. Raymond Klibansky (London, 1949), the latter being more complete. His apologia includes a number of interesting reflections on the history of Fascism in general as well as a bitter denunciation of the House of Savoy's "dyarchy" relationship with the Fascist regime.

A royal dictatorship composed of King Victor Emmanuel III and Marshal Pietro Badoglio was in control of Italy from the coup d'état until the announcement on September 8, 1943, of the armistice with the Allies. Two journalistic books provide lengthy accounts of this period: Melton S. Davis, *Who Defends Rome? The Forty-Five Days, July 25 - September 8, 1943* (New York, 1972); and Ruggero Zangrandi, *1943: 25 luglio - 8 settembre* (Milan, 1964). Mario Toscano's informative monograph on Italian diplomacy is entitled *Dal 25 luglio all'8 settembre* (Florence, 1966). Marshal Badoglio's self-serving memoirs, *Italy in the Second World War* (London, 1948), deal with a longer span. An excellent biography of this military figure who headed the government during the "45 days" and then fled to the South where he and the King were propped up by the Allies has now been published by Piero Pieri and Giorgio Rochat, *Pietro Badoglio* (Turin, 1974). On the King's role in this period, one can turn to the biography by Sergio Bertoldi, cited earlier, and to General Paolo Puntoni, *Parla Vittorio Emanuele III* (Milan, 1958). A very hostile account is *Fall of the House of Savoy* (New York, 1971), by Robert Katz.

A major scholarly work, *The Brutal Friendship: Mussolini, Hitler and the Fall of Italian Fascism* (New York, 1962), has been written by Sir F. William Deakin. It is based on a vast number of documents that were captured by the Allies (the St. Antony's College collection at Oxford). The author provides an excellent account of the Duce's shifting relationship with Hitler between 1942 and 1945. There are good chapters on the coup d'état, but the major contribution of Deakin's book lies in its discussion of Mussolini's activities after he was rescued from the Gran Sasso by the Nazi, Otto Skorzeny, in September 1943 and installed by Hitler as the head of a puppet regime in the German-held northern half of Italy. This was to be the Italian Social Republic—or the "Republic of Salò," as it was derisively christened by its enemies. Salò was on Lake Garda, close to the Germans' main land artery to Italy over the Brenner Pass.

Mussolini was compelled to hold a trial in Verona in January 1944 for the "traitors" who had voted against him in the Grand Council meeting of July 24/25, 1943. Among those condemned to death and shot was Ciano. Meanwhile, Mussolini desperately sought to gain support from the working class by reviving some of the radical and "socialist" trappings that had characterized Fascism in its "first hour" in 1919. But the chief role of the unpopular republic was to engage in bitter warfare against the partisan forces of the Armed Resistance. Deakin's book will long remain of value, though its many pages of documents quoted *in extenso* may put off the casual reader. Other recent books on this topic include Silvio Bertoldi, *Salò: Vita e morte della Repubblica sociale italiana* (Milan, 1976), and Giorgio Bocca, *La repubblica di Mussolini* (Rome, 1977).

Armistice and Co-belligerency

The most authoritative study of the complicated negotiations that led to the surrender of Italy to the Allies and to the announcement of this action on the eve of the Allied invasion at Salerno (September 8, 1943) is *Sicily and the Surrender of Italy* (Washington, 1965), written by Lt. Col. Albert N. Gardner and Howard McGaw Smyth, with the assistance of Martin Blumenson. This is a volume in the official "United States Army in World War II, Mediterranean Theater of Operations" series. It is supplemented from the British side by the second and third volumes of Sir Llewellyn Woodward's *British Foreign Policy in the Second World War* (London, 1971). In October 1943 the Anglo-Americans succeeded in getting the government of the King and Badoglio to declare war on Hitler's Germany. The Allies permitted Italy to enjoy the intermediate status of "co-belligerency." The degree to which Italy "worked her passage back," in Churchill's phrase, would influence the terms of the eventual peace treaty. While the Allies made immediate use of the Italian navy, the British seemed to be in no hurry to re-equip and train the bedraggled Italian soldiers in the South. Eventually, however, an Italian Corps of Liberation (CIL) was outfitted and it rendered good account of itself in 1944/45. *Naples '44* (New York, 1979), based on the diary kept by Norman Lewis, a member of the British Field Security Police, offers a striking description of the terrible living conditions for Italians in that great port city, which became the Allies' major supply base.

Among the official American histories of military aspects of the Italian campaign are Martin Blumenson, *Salerno to Cassino* (Washington, 1969), and Ernest F. Fisher, Jr., *Cassino to the Alps* (Washington, 1977). From the British side, the volumes by Michael Howard and John Ehrman in James R. M. Butler, ed., *Grand Strategy*, 6 vols. (London, 1956-76), supplemented by Howard's shorter study, *The Mediterranean Strategy in the Second World War* (New York, 1968), are all essential. Of interest, too, are a couple of books by British Major General William G. F. Jackson, *The Battle for Italy* (New York, 1967) and *The Battle for Rome* (London, 1969). An American journalist, Dan Kurzman, has written a lively account, *The Race for Rome* (Garden City, N.Y., 1975).

Churchill supported the government of Badoglio and the King because it had signed the armistice. But it was a weak government of technicians. It included no representatives of the anti-Fascist parties that had grouped themselves into the CLNs (Committees of National Liberation). They remained in bitter opposition throughout the winter. Not until the spring of 1944 did the situation change, when suddenly Palmiro Togliatti, leader of the Italian Communists, returned from Moscow with a radically new set of instructions (the *svolta* of Salerno). To the consternation of his fellow Communists as well as the other parties in the CLN, Togliatti declared that his own party was ready to enter the Badoglio government so that the war effort could be strengthened. Togliatti's action forced most of the other CLN parties to do likewise, so that a new government was announced by Badoglio in April. About the same time the Anglo-Americans decided that the controversial Victor Emmanuel must step aside in favor of his son, Crown Prince Umberto, who would assume the title of Lieutenant General of the Realm at the moment Rome was liberated. Victor Emmanuel acquiesced only under protest.

When Rome was emancipated early in June 1944, however, most of the anti-Fascist politicians, including even Togliatti, made it clear to Premier Badoglio that they were no longer prepared to support him. Instead, they asked Ivanoe Bonomi, an elderly former premier (1921-22) who had been the nominal head of the clandestine CLN in Rome during the German occupation, to become the new head of government. Bonomi's *Diario di un anno, 2 giugno 1943 - 10 giugno 1944* (Milan, 1947), is a primary source of information for this period.[19] Churchill was incensed that Badoglio had been cast aside but was compelled to accept it. Within a few weeks it became increasingly evident that Premier Bonomi was promonarchist. As a result, the strongly republican-minded Socialist and Action parties withdrew from the government in November 1944, forcing him to reorganize it. Many Italians would have preferred to see Count Carlo Sforza, a one-time foreign minister who had returned from years of exile, become premier (and the Americans would have been happy with him), but Churchill resolutely vetoed Sforza because of his antimonarchist stance.

Allied military government in Italy was dominated by British policymakers during the first year or so. The official British history is Charles R. S. Harris, *Allied Military Administration of Italy, 1943–1945* (London, 1957). The major official American account is a documentary work edited by Harry L. Coles and Albert K. Weinberg, *Civil Affairs: Soldiers Become Governors* (Washington, 1964). Writing from a left-wing perspective, David W. Ellwood, a British historian, has recently brought out a sharply revisionist criticism of many British policies: *L'alleato nemico: La politica dell'occupazione anglo-americana in Italia, 1943–1946* (Milan, 1977). Harold Macmillan's memoirs, *The Blast of War, 1939–1945* (New York, 1967), contain interesting sections on his role as a policymaker in Italy. Some additional information, from an Italian perspective, may be found in Lamberto Mercuri's book, *1943–1945: Gli alleati e l'Italia* (Naples, 1975).

Norman Kogan's *Italy and the Allies* (Cambridge, Mass., 1956) is a concise analysis of the three-cornered relationship among the British, the Americans, and the Italian governments, as well as of Allied policies in the peace settlement of 1947. Further elucidation of Allied policy, particularly as it developed in Naples between September 1943 and June 1944, is contained in Benedetto Croce's fascinating diary, *Croce, the King, and the Allies,* ed. Sylvia Sprigge (New York, 1950). Croce was at the hub of many of the discussions over what to do with the stubborn Victor Emmanuel, whose continuing occupancy of the throne was a major impediment to national unity.

---

[19]Bonomi also wrote several works of history, including *From Socialism to Fascism: A Study of Contemporary Italy* (London, 1924); *La politica italiana da Porta Pia a Vittorio Veneto* (Turin, 1944); and *La politica italiana dopo Vittorio Veneto* (Turin, 1955).

Armed Resistance, 1943-1945

Italy's Armed Resistance was an anti-German, anti-Fascist struggle that took place in the northern half of the peninsula from September 8, 1943, until April 25, 1945. In addition to the guerrilla warfare, there was much passive resistance to the enemy. Resisters included remnants of the Italian armed forces that had been quickly overpowered by the Germans in the confusion surrounding the announcement of the armistice. These were supplemented by large numbers of men who were anxious to avoid military and labor conscription by the enemy, and by numerous staunch anti-Fascists who had come out into the open after the coup d'état and whose lives were consequently in danger. Resisters came from all walks of life but were especially numerous among the peasantry, workers, and professional people. Many lower clergy and women were also involved. The partisan armed units usually preferred to operate from bases in the foothills and mountains. In the cities Socialists and Communists gave much attention to organizing factory workers. The Communists also recruited young boys into terrorist units (Gappisti).

From the outset, the Resistance consisted of two wings: (1) the "autonomous" units, made up initially from disbanded elements of the Italian Army and who tended to be cautious in their military strategy and supportive of the Royal government in the South; and (2) the more politically activist wing, identified with the Communist, Socialist, and Action parties and the new CLN's. The latter sector was the stronger; it called for vigorous guerrilla warfare and radical renovation of Italy's political and economic structure. Most members of this category favored a republic based on the new five-party CLN's and an economy that would be socialized to a considerable extent. They were willing to defer the thorny issue of Church-State relations. The American OSS (Office of Strategic Services) and the British SOE (Special Operations Executive) gave significant material and financial support to the resisters, particularly after the liberation of Rome and Florence in mid-1944. They parachuted liaison officers into the North to help coordinate operations and to try to maintain a rough equilibrium among the various factions. But tensions between the Allies and resisters remained near the surface, especially in the late autumn of 1944 after the British experienced much difficulty in Greece with left-wing partisans who refused to accept the return of the monarchy. Hoping to forestall trouble with Italian partisans at the moment of liberation, the Allies invited representatives from the Milan CLNAI (CLN for Upper Italy) to come to Allied headquarters in Caserta, where they persuaded them to sign an important agreement on December 7, 1944. In return for Allied promises of arms and money, the CLNAI promised to obey all orders issued by the Allies, including that of surrendering their weapons at war's end. About the same time, the Bonomi government in Rome agreed to recognize the CLNAI as its "delegate" in the North.

The Allies at last were able to break through the Apennines into the Po valley early in April 1945. Resistance fighters played a major role in liberating the Apennine-Liguria region, Genoa, Bologna, Milan, Turin, and Venice. In Genoa and Venice they safeguarded port facilities. Throughout the North they helped prevent the enemy from carrying out "scorch" policies. On April 25 Mussolini belatedly sought to bargain with the CLNAI in Milan but soon decided to flee, hoping to escape to Switzerland. Partisans captured him and other hierarchs at a roadblock alongside Lake Como on the 27th. He and his mistress Clara Petacci were executed the next day.

Altogether, 250,000 Italians took part in the Armed Resistance. Casualties were high, exceeding those of the Allied forces in Italy. To some 36,000 partisans killed on Italian soil must be added 10,000 Italian civilians killed in reprisals, while some 10,000 Italian soldiers fighting alongside the Allied forces fell in combat. Another 32,000 Italians died fighting in foreign Resistance movements, while a similar number were killed in German internment camps. Some 8,000 Jews were deported from Italy and killed by the Germans.

On the Armed Resistance one has Delzell's major study, *Mussolini's Enemies,* cited earlier, and the first-hand observations of Massimo Salvadori, who was the British liaison officer at the CLNAI in Milan in 1945: "The Patriot Movement in Italy," *Foreign Affairs* 24 (Apr. 1946): 539–49, supplemented, in Italian, by his book, *Breve storia della Resistenza italiana* (reprinted, Florence, 1974). There are three classic accounts by Italian participants: *Un popolo alla macchia* (Milan, 1947), by the Communist military leader, Luigi Longo; *Tutte le strade conducono a Roma* (Florence, 1947), by a key Action party leader, Leo Valiani; and *La Riscossa: Dal 25 luglio alla liberazione* (Milan, 1948), by General Raffaele Cadorna, the professional Italian Army officer sent to the North by Bonomi to help coordinate the Resistance. Needless to say, almost every major figure in the Resistance has written about some aspect of the period. The first attempt to write a comprehensive history was Roberto Battaglia's detailed *Storia della Resistenza italiana* (2d ed., Turin, 1953), which, despite its Communist slant, remains a helpful contribution and provides a detailed bibliography broken down by regions. An abridged English version has been published: *Story of the Italian Resistance* (London, 1957). Renato Carli-Ballola, *Storia della Resistenza* (Milan, 1957), interprets it from the Socialist party's standpoint. Giorgio Bocca, *Storia dell'Italia partigiana, settembre 1943 – maggio 1945* (Bari, 1966), is a good popular account. An outstanding study of the three major political forces in the Resistance, *Azionisti, cattolici e comunisti nella Resistenza* (Milan, 1971), has been written by knowledgeable scholars in each current: Leo Valiani, Gianfranco Bianchi, and Ernesto Ragionieri. Specialists will also want to consult Guido Quazza's important work, *Resistenza e storia d'Italia: Problemi e ipotesi di ricerca* (Milan, 1976), which suggests many topics that still need investigation. The recently released official OSS history, *The Overseas Targets: War Report of the OSS (Office of Strategic Services)*, Vol. 2, (New York and Washington, 1976), includes a section on the Italian Resistance.[20] Under the auspices of the University Institute of European Studies in Turin, David W. Ellwood and James E. Miller have compiled a helpful *Introductory Guide to American Documentation of the European Resistance Movements in World War II: Public Records* (Turin, 1975).

In their book *Operation Sunrise: The Secret Surrender* (New York, 1979), Bradley F. Smith and Elena Agarossi deal judiciously with the controversial armistice negotiations undertaken by the German SS commander in Italy, General Karl Wolff, with Allen W. Dulles, the OSS agent in Switzerland, to end the war in Italy in the spring of 1945. These secret talks aroused much suspicion on the part of Stalin, who apparently feared that Allied forces might thereby be enabled to capture Trieste before Tito's Yugoslav Partisans could. It turned out that the Yugoslavs reached Trieste a few hours before

---

[20]Charles F. Delzell has drawn upon this for his paper, "The American OSS and the Italian Armed Resistance," in Centro Studi Formazioni Autonome del Piemonte, *Atti del convegno internazionale, Missioni alleate e partigiani autonomi, Torino, 21–22 ottobre 1978*, ed. Renzo Amedeo (Turin, 1980), pp. 353–97.

Allied troops did, as Geoffrey Cox, a New Zealand army intelligence officer who was personally involved, explains in *The Race for Trieste* (London, 1977). The status of Trieste was to remain in dispute with Yugoslavia for many years after the war.

Howard McGaw Smyth, *Secrets of the Fascist Era: How Uncle Sam Obtained Some of the Top-Level Documents of Mussolini's Period* (Carbondale, 1975), written by a former historian in the U.S. State Department, tells the fascinating story of how Count Ciano's diaries and other important Fascist documents came into Allied hands during the war.

Postwar Political Patterns

By the time the liberation of the Po valley occurred in April 1945, everyone sensed that the leftist-oriented political forces of the Armed Resistance in the industrialized North would have to be accommodated in a new Italian government. Protracted negotiations between the Resistance leaders from Milan with the politicians in Rome resulted in a deadlock among the three *partiti di massa:* Communists, Socialists, and Christian Democrats. At last, they compromised by permitting Ferruccio Parri, a respected leader in the North of the smaller Action party, to form a government.[21] Parri was acceptable to the Allies, who had negotiated with him the December 7, 1944, Caserta accords with the CLNAI. The Parri government, lasting from June until December 1945, marked the farthest to the left that Italian politics swung in the postwar period. But the role of the CLNs disappeared rapidly after Allied Military Government was established temporarily in the North and the traditional prefectural, centralized administrative structure was reinstated. Parri struggled doggedly with the desperate economic situation, Sicilian separatism, and other problems. But he was compelled, at last, to resign in the face of rising hostility from the conservative-minded Liberals and the Christian Democrats, who objected to the efforts by the leftist parties to continue the purge of Fascists from the bureaucracy.

Alcide De Gasperi, the capable leader of the Christian Democrats, became the new premier. He was to hold this post through a series of eight governments until August 1953. Every government thereafter was also to be headed by a Christian

[21]Parri's collected writings have been published recently: *Scritti 1915-1975* (Milan, 1976), ed. Enzo Collotti, Giorgio Rochat, Gabriella Solaro Pelazza, and Paolo Speziale.

Democrat. Meanwhile, on June 2, 1946, the fate of the House of Savoy was sealed in a referendum in which women also voted for the first time. The republic won by a margin of 12,700,000 to 10,700,000. The North voted solidly for it, while the South cast its ballots just as compactly for retention of the monarchy. As a kind of consolation prize to the South, Enrico De Nicola, a Neapolitan monarchist, was named Provisional President of the Republic. Italians also elected on June 2 the Constituent Assembly, which proceeded to draw up a new constitution in 1947. This document called for a new system of regional governments and a supreme Constitutional Court, but in other respects reinstated a fairly traditional pattern of parliamentary government. Simultaneously in Paris, the Allies were drafting a peace treaty that, in spite of Italian objections, was to deprive that country of all of her colonies, even those she had acquired in the pre-Fascist era. Otherwise the peace treaty was reasonably generous to Italy. And the Americans continued to pour in economic assistance to help rebuild the devastated country.

The first parliamentary elections under the new constitution took place on April 18, 1948. The Christian Democrats won a major triumph, attributable partly to the Cold War tension and fears that Communists might try to replicate in Italy the seizure of power they had carried out in Czechoslovakia in February. For the next five years, the Christian Democrats held a clear majority in parliament. In the face of this political stabilization, many of the idealistic dreams of reform engendered during the Resistance era tended to fade away. There was even a short-lived recrudescence of neo-Fascism under the curious label of the Uomo Qualunque (Common Man party), about which there is a recent monograph by Sandro Setta, *L'Uomo Qualunque, 1944-1948* (Bari, 1975).

Although a good deal of economic reconstruction took place and some overdue land reform measures were carried out in Calabria, Sicily, and elsewhere, De Gasperi's eight years as premier were noteworthy less for domestic renovation than for aligning Italy solidly with the West in the Cold War. Italy was a charter member of the Marshall Plan's OEEC (Organization for European Economic Cooperation) and also of NATO (North Atlantic Treaty Organization). Italy's admission to the United Nations, however, was delayed until 1955 because of the East-West deadlock.[22]

[22]Three volumes of the *Discorsi parlamentari di Alcide De Gasperi* (Rome, 1973), have been published by the Chamber of Deputies. The statesman's daughter, Maria Romana Catti De

De Gasperi was supported in his foreign policy moves by Luigi Einaudi, an eminent liberal economist from Turin who was elected by parliament to fill the office of President of the Republic, 1948-1955. Both of them were strong believers in European economic and political integration. Many of the writings of Einaudi during the years of his presidency are collected in his *Lo scrittoio del presidente, 1948-1955* (Turin, 1956). Enrico Decleva is writing a biography of him for the Valeri series.

Among the contemporary Italian accounts of the political shifts that took place during the immediate postwar period were Giulio Andreotti's *Concerto a sei voci* (Rome, 1945) and Leo Valiani's able study, *L'avvento di De Gasperi: Tre anni di politica italiana* (Turin, 1949). Later studies of this period include Raffaele Colapietra, *La lotta politica in Italia dalla liberazione di Roma alla Costituente* (Bologna, 1969); Enzo Piscitelli, *Da Parri a De Gasperi* (Milan, 1975); and Antonio Gambino, *Storia del dopoguerra dalla liberazione al potere DC* (Bari, 1975).

English-language studies focusing on these early postwar years include the comparative study, *Christian Democracy in Italy and France* (Notre Dame, 1952), by Mario Einaudi, a professor of government at Cornell University who was, incidentally, a son of Luigi Einaudi, the Italian President; *The Rebuilding of Italy: Politics and Economics, 1945-1955* (London, 1955), by Muriel Grindrod, a well-informed British observer; *Italy after Fascism: A Political History, 1943-1963* (Montreal, 1964), by Giuseppe Mammarella, a political scientist who prepared his book from lectures presented to American students at Stanford-in-Florence; and *The Rebirth of Italy, 1943-50* (London, 1972), edited by Stuart J. Woolf and containing a number of essays by British and Italian specialists, the most satisfactory of which are by himself and Franco Catalano.

Probably the best place to start in English, however, is with the broad studies by H. Stuart Hughes and Norman Kogan. Hughes's book, *The United States and Italy* (3rd rev. ed., Cambridge, Mass., 1979), has been mentioned before. It surveys politics, international relations, economics, social structure, and cultural trends, giving

---

Gasperi, has written *De Gasperi, uomo solo* (Verona, 1964). A party colleague, Giulio Andreotti, has published *De Gasperi e il suo tempo* (Milan, 1965) and an *Intervista su De Gasperi* (Bari, 1977). A major biography is being prepared for the Valeri series by Pietro Scoppola, who has already published a shorter study, *La proposta politica di De Gasperi* (Bologna, 1977).

particular emphasis to the postwar period. In the most recent edition, Hughes has interesting new sections on Italy's economic expansion and entry into the Common Market; the cultural renaissance; the nation's role in the Western community; an analysis of the status of Italian women and their successful drive to legalize divorce and abortion; an evaluation of Italy's so-called "ill-developed society"; and a discussion of the proposals by Enrico Berlinguer's Communist party in the late 1970s for a "historic compromise" with the Christian Democrats. Kogan, an American political scientist, has been a close observer of the Italian scene and has interviewed many of its politicians. His two-volume study is entitled *A Political History of Postwar Italy* (New York, 1966 and 1981). The earlier volume deals chiefly with the De Gasperi era and the ensuing decade of political immobilism (1953-63). The sequel is subtitled *From the Old to the New Center Left, 1965-1980*.

Italy's immobilism was brought about by that country's intractable political divisions: the seemingly irreducible strength of the opposition Communist-Socialist bloc on the Left and of the neo-Fascist and Monarchist bloc on the extreme Right. Among the Christian Democratic premiers in the post-De Gasperi decade were Giuseppe Pella, Amintore Fanfani, Mario Scelba, Antonio Segni, Adone Zoli, and Fernando Tambroni. The last-named prime minister unwisely sought to win the backing of the neo-Fascists and Monarchists in an "opening to the Right" in the spring of 1960. Tambroni was forced to back down when it appeared as if civil war might result. The decade of "immobilism" saw the Presidency of the Republic occupied by two Christian Democrats: Giovanni Gronchi (1955-62), a Catholic labor leader from Tuscany; and Antonio Segni (1962-64), a Sardinian politician who was forced to resign because of ill health. All of these and many later developments are discussed at length in Giorgio Galli's *Storia della Democrazia Cristiana* (Bari, 1978), one of the better Italian studies of this major political party.

The possibility for a breakout from the stalemate situation occurred in 1956, when Soviet Russia's brutal suppression of the Hungarian revolution alienated Italian Socialists, causing them to break away from their Communist partners. The advent of a new pope in 1958, John XXIII, was also of some help in reducing the Vatican's hostility toward the Left. The emerging political bloc that came to power in Italy in 1963 was what Kogan terms the "old

Center Left." It came into being when Pietro Nenni's Socialists were ready to respond, for a price, to the almost desperate invitations they received from such Christian Democrats as Fanfani and Aldo Moro to enter the government. The Socialists' price included nationalization of the electric power industry, major tax reforms, and implementation of the Constitution's neglected provisions for regional governments throughout the peninsula. (Hitherto, they had been implemented only in the islands of Sicily and Sardinia and in the northern frontier regions of the Val d'Aosta, Trentino-Alto Adige, and Friuli-Venezia Giulia.) Economic difficulties in the mid-1960s took some of the luster off this "opening to the Left" (*apertura a sinistra*) and contributed to its eventual dissolution. Meanwhile, in the years after 1963, the premiership rotated among the Christian Democrats Aldo Moro, Giovanni Leone, Mariano Rumor, Emilio Colombo, Giulio Andreotti, Francesco Cossiga, and Arnaldo Forlani. The office of President of the Republic saw greater political diversity among its occupants, however. Thus, the term of the Social Democrat, Giuseppe Saragat (1964-71), was followed by that of Giovanni Leone, a Christian Democrat (1971-78). When President Leone was forced to resign in disgrace in the face of charges that he had been implicated in kickbacks from the Lockheed Aircraft Corporation, an 81-year-old Socialist party veteran of Fascist prisons and exile, Sandro Pertini, was elected to that office in the summer of 1978.

The "new" Center Left began to develop in the late 1970s when Berlinguer's Communists sought to work out a de facto partnership with the faction-ridden Christian Democrats. It collapsed in 1979 in the wake of electoral setbacks for the Communists after the kidnapping and murder of Aldo Moro (as will be discussed later). Thereafter, it was to be the Socialist party, now under the leadership of Bettino Craxi and divested of much of its old Marxist rhetoric, that worked out a bargain with the Christian Democrats, a bargain which the Socialists hoped would enable them to play the role of "kingmaker" in Italy's volatile political arena.

A good explanation of the complicated history of the strifetorn Socialist party in the postwar years is presented by Giorgio Spini in *Trent'anni di politica socialista (1946-1976): Atti del convegno di Parma organizzato dall'Istituto socialista di studi storici* (Rome, 1977). Giuseppe Tamburanno's interview with the late Pietro Nenni, *Intervista sul socialismo italiano* (Bari, 1977), is also sprinkled with knowledgeable comments about the party's history.

Italy's very recent political and social trends may also be followed in *Italy in the 1970s* (London, 1975), by John Earle, a London *Times* newspaperman stationed in Rome; and in Peter Lange and Sidney Tarrow, eds., *Italy in Transition: Conflict and Consensus* (London, 1980). The latter is based on a symposium in which Italian scholars and others participated. The majority expressed some confidence that Italian democracy, having survived so many other crises, would eventually develop stability.

Peter Lange, it may be noted, has also compiled a useful reference guide to the social science literature in English: *Studies on Italy, 1943-1975: Select Bibliography of American and British Materials in Political Science, Economics, Sociology, and Anthropology* (Turin, 1977). It is unfortunate that Lange's guide was apparently hastily prepared and includes a number of errors. It is especially helpful, however, for its references to dissertations. Listings are broken down into many subcategories. No works by historians or journalists are included.

For a clarification of the constitutional and institutional structure of postwar Italy, one can recommend the following handbooks: Dante Germino and Stefano Passigli, *The Government and Politics of Contemporary Italy* (New York, 1968); older ones by John Clarke Adams and Paolo Barile, *The Government of Republican Italy* (Boston, 1961); and Norman Kogan, *The Government of Italy* (New York, 1962). A ground-breaking history of the bureaucracy and prefectures has been written by the political scientist Robert C. Fried, *The Italian Prefects: A Study in Administrative Politics* (New Haven, 1963). *Interest Groups in Italian Politics* (Princeton, 1964), by Joseph La Palombara, seeks to apply empirically to the Italian political setting some of the concepts developed in America regarding interest group behavior. Among the groups La Palombara has studied are the General Confederation of Italian Industry, Catholic Action, the Christian Democrats, the Liberal, Monarchist, and Republican parties, and the neo-Fascist Italian Social Movement (MSI). Still another political scientist, Giuseppe Di Palma, has sought to analyze the content and procedures of Italian parliamentary legislation in *Surviving Without Governing: The Italian Parties in Parliament* (Berkeley, 1977). The author's findings apply best to the 1950s and 1960s.

Sidney Tarrow has written an instructive comparative study, *Between Center and Periphery: Grassroots Politicians in Italy and France* (New Haven, 1977). A sociologist, Gianfranco Poggi, has made a detailed examination of the structure of *Catholic Action in Italy: The Sociology of a Sponsored Organization* (Stanford, 1967). Giorgio Galli and Alfonso Prandi, research directors of the Carlo Cattaneo Institute in Bologna, have coauthored *Patterns of Political Participation in Italy* (New Haven, 1970). A statistical analysis of the 1968 parliamentary elections can be found in the political scientist Samuel H. Barnes's little book, *Representation in Italy: Institutionalized Tradition and Electoral Choice* (Chicago, 1977).

In the field of urban history and politics, three recent works in English have appeared. Robert C. Fried has written a first-rate account of urban renewal and proposals for further development of Italy's capital: *Planning the Eternal City: Roman Politics and Planning Since World War II* (New Haven, 1973). A British scholar, P. A. Allum, has done a good job on Italy's southern metropolis: *Politics and Society in Postwar Naples* (Cambridge, Eng., 1973). He is also the author of *Italy, Republic Without Government* (London, 1973). Robert H. Evans has made a close investigation of *Life and Politics in a Venetian Community* (Notre Dame, 1976), in which he examines the transformation of a village between 1866 and 1972, giving emphasis to the Fascist and postwar periods.

Communism in Italy

The Italian Communist party (PCI), which has emerged since the war as the strongest challenger of the ruling Christian Democratic party, has attracted a great deal of scholarly attention, not only in analyzing the circumstances of its separation from the Socialist party in 1921 and in recounting the vicissitudes it suffered during the Fascist era, but in seeking to explain the reasons for its very rapid growth after 1943. By the late 1960s the party archives were opened, making possible the detailed study by the Communist historian, Paolo Spriano, whose five-volume work, *Storia del Partito comunista italiano* (Turin, 1967-76), covers the period 1921-1945. Spriano is remarkably candid in elucidating issues that have long been shrouded in polemics. A non-Communist, Giuseppe Mammarella, has written a much shorter account of the postwar period: *Partito comunista italiano, 1945-1974* (Florence, 1976).

The principal intellectual founder of the PCI, Antonio Gramsci (born in Sardinia in 1891; died of tuberculosis in Rome, 1937, after a decade of Fascist imprisonment), has aroused an immense amount of interest both in Italy and abroad. This is partly because of the posthumous publication of his collected works, "Opere di Antonio Gramsci" (Turin, 1947-58), including his prison notebooks, which point up his sometimes independent-minded, "Western"-style Marxism. Available in English are *Selections from the Prison Notebooks of Antonio Gramsci* (New York, 1971), eds. Quintin Hoare and Geoffrey N. Smith; *Letters from Prison* (New York, 1973), ed. Lynne Lawner; and Gramsci's *The Modern Prince and Other Writings* (New York, 1959).

There are many studies of Gramsci's thought and actions. John H. Cammett, an American Marxist, has written on *Antonio Gramsci and the Origins of Italian Communism* (Stanford, 1967), as has Martin Clark in *Antonio Gramsci and the Revolution that Failed* (New Haven, 1977). A lengthy biography by Salvatore Francesco Romano, *Antonio Gramsci* (Turin, 1967), sheds some light on his Turin years. *Antonio Gramsci: Life of a Revolutionary* (New York, 1971), by the Italian journalist Giuseppe Fiori, is revealing about his Sardinian childhood and his misgivings about Stalinism. The British scholar, James Joll, takes a broad perspective in his succinct book, *Antonio Gramsci* (New York, 1978). John A. Davis, ed., *Gramsci and Italy's Passive Revolution* (London, 1979), contains essays by seven Anglo-American specialists who explore various aspects of the economic and social structure of the early twentieth-century Italian liberal state. Rosario Romeo, a staunchly liberal historian, has sharply challenged the Gramscian school of Marxian historiography in essays collected in *Italia moderna fra storia e storiografia* (Bari, 1977) and *L'Italia unita e la prima guerra mondiale* (Bari, 1978).

A long biography, *Palmiro Togliatti* (Bari, 1973), by the journalist Giorgio Bocca, has been written about Gramsci's successor as leader of the PCI from the late 1920s until his death in 1964. Togliatti came out openly in favor of "polycentrist" Communism in 1956 at the time of the Soviet suppression of the Hungarian revolution. His collected writings, *Opere* (Rome, 1973 ff.), are being edited by Ernesto Ragionieri. Togliatti's principal successor was his protégé, Enrico Berlinguer, a native of Sardinia and leader of the party's youth movement in the early postwar years. The journalist Vittorio Gorresio has published a brief profile, *Berlinguer* (Milan, 1976).

David I. Kertzer, *Comrades and Christians: Religion and Political Struggle in Communist Italy* (Cambridge, Eng., 1980), examines the popular basis of Communism's influence, focusing on the rivalry between the Party and the Church. Belden Paulson, with the help of Athos Ricci, has written *The Searchers: Conflict and Communism in an Italian Town* (Chicago, 1966), which also examines the popular appeal of Communism at the grassroots level—in this case, by interviewing a cross section of the inhabitants of an anonymous town in the Alban hills near Rome. Another useful study of Communism at the local level is Robert H. Evans, *Coexistence: Communism and Its Practice in Bologna, 1945-1965* (Notre Dame, 1967). It discusses the generally efficient role of the Communist municipal government in this "Red citadel" where the party has been in control since 1945.

On the relationship of the PCI to other Communist forces in Europe a number of books can be mentioned. An early study was Mario Einaudi, Aldo Garosci, and J. M. Domenach, *Communism in Western Europe* (Ithaca, 1951). William E. Griffith, ed., *Communism in Europe: Continuity, Change and the Sino-Soviet Dispute* (Cambridge, Mass., 1964), emphasizes the repercussions in Europe of the breakup of monolithic Communism when Mao Zedong's China severed ideological ties with Soviet Russia in 1960-62. The book contains a chapter on the PCI by Giorgio Galli, an ex-Communist. Donald L. M. Blackmer has written *Unity in Diversity: Italian Communism and the Communist World* (Cambridge, Mass., 1968), and has coauthored with Sidney Tarrow *Communism in Italy and France* (Princeton, 1975). Several other comparative studies are William E. Griffith, ed., *The European Left: Italy, France, and Spain* (Lexington, Mass., 1979), which contains chapters on Italy written by himself, Wolfgang Berner, Giuseppe Sacco, and Stefano Silvestri; and David E. Albright, ed., *Communism and Political Systems in Western Europe* (Boulder, 1979), which includes a chapter on Italy by Giacomo Sani; Morton A. Kaplan, *The Many Faces of Communism* (New York, 1978), with a chapter on Italy by the Italian sociologist Franco Ferrarotti; R. Neal Tannahill, *The Communist Parties of Western Europe: A Comparative Study* (Westport, Conn., 1978); and Neil McInnes, *The Communist Parties of Western Europe* (London, 1975).

The concept of Eurocommunism, which Enrico Berlinguer was to push vigorously after the mid-1970s, is discussed with some degree of optimism in Norman Kogan's chapter in *Eurocommunism and Détente,* ed. Rudolph L. Tökés (New York, 1978), a Council on Foreign Relations book. It is viewed with more skepticism in George R. Urban, ed., *Eurocommunism: Its Roots and Future in Italy and Elsewhere* (New York, 1978), a collection of interviews he held on Radio Free Europe in 1977 with such Italians as Lucio Lombardo-Radice, Fabio Mussi, Altiero Spinelli, and Luigi Barzini; and in *Eurocommunism: The Italian Case* (Washington, 1978), ed. Austin Ranney and Giovanni Sartori, based on a conference sponsored jointly by the American Enterprise Institute for Public Policy Research and the Hoover Institution on War, Revolution and Peace. Other books worthy of mention are Wolfgang Leonhard, *Eurocommunism: Challenge for East and West* (New York, 1980); Keith Middlemas, *Power and the Party: Changing Faces of Communism in Western Europe* (London, 1980); and Walter Laqueur's chapter on Eurocommunism in his *A Continent Astray: Europe 1970–1978* (New York, 1979).

Closely linked to Eurocommunism has been Berlinguer's call for a "historic compromise" with Italy's Christian Democrats that would enable the Communists to share some of the ministries. Berlinguer developed this proposal in the light of Salvador Allende's fatal experience in Chile, where his Marxist government was overthrown in 1973 when it tried to govern without the cooperation of the Catholics. Thus far, the proposed "historic compromise" has been resisted by the right wing of the Italian DC party, the Vatican, and the United States. But Aldo Moro and Giulio Andreotti of the center-left wing of Christian Democracy did work out some ingenious procedures in 1977/78 for consultation with the Communists, though stopping short of letting them into the cabinet. Subsequently, however, that arrangement broke down.

Urban Terrorism

In the years after the university upheavals of 1968/69 and the ensuing "hot summer" of labor unrest, terrorism spread like wildfire through Italy. There was a kind of pendulum swing to the terror. During the first part of the 1970s the terrorists emerged chiefly from the neo-Fascist Right; they murdered some forty people and injured many more. During the last half of the 1970s the pendulum swung in the opposite direction. Better organized and more widely supported sharpshooters of such extreme leftist groups as the Red Brigades killed about 150 people and "kneecapped" many others. By 1980, as left-wing terrorism appeared to falter under the crackdown of a reorganized police force, there was a swing back toward "Black" terrorism. The seemingly senseless bombing of the Bologna railway station in August 1980 killed 80 people and injured nearly 200 others in the worst single act of political violence to take place in Western Europe since World War II.

A number of journalists and social scientists have sought to explain the aims of the Red Brigades and their counterparts on the extreme Right. Among the explanations are that terrorism is basically a sick reaction to a society that cannot easily adapt to change. This seems especially true in a country like Italy where a single party, the Christian Democratic, in power since 1945, has been unable to renew itself. For the Christian Democrats, power seems to have become an end in itself, resulting in corruption, inefficiency, and paternalism. Its clerical-conservative groups seek to impose values on a society that is able neither fully to accept them nor, because of the immutability of power, to evolve alternatives. The terrorists have likewise denounced the Communist party for its "sellout" in seeking to gain a partnership role in government. Many of the arms used by the terrorists appear to come from Communist Czechoslovakia, which may have a stake in trying to destabilize Italy. There is some speculation that the Palestinian Liberation Organization and Libyan Republic may also be involved in supplying the arms. The victims in Italy have usually been industrialists, prosecuting attorneys, judges, police officials and politicians, though in the case of the Bologna bombing there seemed to be no precise target. The most publicized atrocity was the brutal kidnapping and murder in Rome in the spring of 1978 of Aldo Moro, a former Christian Democratic premier—a crime which led the government to redouble its efforts to eliminate the terrorists.

Among the studies of the terrorist phenomenon are Giorgio Bocca, *Il terrorismo italiano, 1970–1978* (Milan, 1978); and Alessandro Silj, *Never Again Without a Rifle: The Origins of Italian Terrorism* (New York, 1979), which draws upon a number of interviews with radical leftists who became terrorists and were later convicted and sentenced, e.g., Renato Curcio and Roberto Ognibene. Walter Laqueur, *Terrorism* (London, 1977), is a broader study of the terrorist phenomenon in several countries. Robert Katz, in *The Ordeal of Aldo Moro: The Kidnapping, the Execution, the Aftermath* (New York, 1980), does a good job describing the circumstances and repercussions of that crime. The author is on shakier ground, however, when he condemns the Christian Democratic government of Andreotti for its refusal to negotiate with the Red Brigades in 1978.

Church and State in the Postwar Period

Giulio Andreotti alludes to some of the above problems in a fascinating, anecdotal account of his personal association with six pontiffs from the 1920s to the 1970s: *A ogni morte di papa* (Milan, 1980). Under pressure from his own DC party as well as from the PCI in 1978, Premier Andreotti resisted Pope Paul VI's efforts to have the government make some concessions to the Red Brigades in order to save the life of their mutual friend, Moro, a friendship that went back to their university days in Milan.

Andreotti is also informative about the pontificates of Pius XI (1922–39), Pius XII (1939–1958), and John XXIII (1958–1963). So is the anticlerical historian, Carlo Falconi, in *The Popes in the Twentieth Century: From Pius X to John XXIII* (London, 1967). Papa Pacelli (Pius XII),[23] the urbane Roman aristocrat, exercised a great deal of influence on Italian politics in the postwar years, Andreotti observes, while John XXIII, jovial and generous, was more than a match for the craftiest of Italian politicians. The brief reign of John Paul I in the late summer of 1978 was scarcely long enough for Andreotti to take his measure. The advent thereafter of the Polish pope, John Paul II, has perhaps ushered in a new era, one in which the Vatican may not choose to let itself become quite so intimately involved in Italian politics as before, though one cannot be sure of this.

The terms of the Lateran Concordat of 1929 were offensive to advocates of separation of Church and State. Such groups were dismayed when the concordat was made an integral part of the Constitution of the Italian Republic in 1947, thanks to the unexpected support of Palmiro Togliatti, who presumed (mistakenly, it turned out) that this action would endear his PCI to the ruling Christian Democrats. In the late 1970s negotiations were begun by the Italian government with the Holy See to revise some of the most objection-

---

[23]Francesco Traniello is writing a biography of Pius XII for the Valeri series.

able provisions. The background of some of these issues is discussed in *Church and State in Italy, 1947-1957* (London, 1958), by an Australian specialist, Leicester C. Webb, and by P. Vincent Bucci, *Chiesa e Stato: Church-State Relations in Italy Within the Contemporary Constitutional Framework* (The Hague, 1969). The Church was, of course, bitterly opposed to Italy's legalization of divorce and abortion in the 1970s.

Postwar Socioeconomic Developments

Although it is poorly organized and sometimes confusing, Shepard B. Clough's *Economic History of Modern Italy* (New York, 1964) seeks to give a comprehensive view of the past century. Kevin Allen and Andrew Stevenson, *An Introduction to the Italian Economy* (New York, 1975), set forth an "economist's history" of the postwar period, emphasizing the recovery from wartime destruction and the advent of the "economic miracle" of the 1950s. Their book ends on a gloomier note, however. "Italy 1920-1970," by Sergio Riscossa, is a succinct account of economic history during Fascism and the subsequent quarter century. It forms chapter 5 in the *Fontana Economic History of Europe,* Vol. VI, Part 1 *(Contemporary Economics),* ed. Carlo M. Cipolla (Glasgow, 1976).

The history and problems of the Italian labor movement have drawn the attention of such social scientists as Joseph La Palombara, *The Italian Labor Movement: Problems and Prospects* (Ithaca, 1957); Maurice F. Neufeld, *Italy, School for Awakening Countries: The Italian Labor Movement in its Political, Social, and Economic Setting from 1800 to 1960* (Ithaca, 1961); and Daniel L. Horowitz, *The Italian Labor Movement* (Cambridge, Mass., 1963).

The IRI (Istituto per la ricostruzione italiana), the state holding company set up by Mussolini in 1933, has continued into the post-Fascist era, so that there is now parastatal involvement of the government in about 30% of Italian industry. This is discussed in Stuart Holland, ed., *The State as Entrepreneur: New Dimensions to Public Enterprise: The IRI State Shareholding Formula* (London, 1972), as well as in M. V. Posner and Stuart J. Woolf, *Italian Public Enterprise* (Cambridge, Mass., 1967) which seeks to vindicate the performance of public enterprise. Two studies of Enrico Mattei, the imaginative entrepreneur who, before his accidental death in 1963, organized the vast parastatal ENI (National Hydrocarbons Board) to develop new sources of energy, have been written by Dow Votaw, *The Six-Legged Dog: Mattei and ENI—A Study in Power* (Berkeley, 1964), and by P. H. Frankel, *Mattei, Oil and Power Politics* (New York, 1966). Other studies pertaining to economic planning and the government's role include Mario Einaudi, Maurice Byé, and Ernesto Rossi, *Nationalization in France and Italy* (Ithaca, 1955); Joseph La Palombara, *Italy: The Politics of Planning* (Syracuse, 1966); George H. Hildebrand, *Growth and Structure in the Economy of Modern Italy* (Cambridge, Mass., 1965); and Vera Lutz, *Italy: A Study in Economic Development* (London, 1962), which takes a critical view of the government's assignment of scarce economic resources.

The South

Italy's problem of a persistently impoverished South was brought forcefully to the attention of northern Italians as well as of foreigners by Carlo Levi's *Christ Stopped at Eboli* (New York, 1947), a brilliant description of peasant mores in Lucania. This Piedmontese physician-artist-novelist was exiled there as a political prisoner in 1935. The title of his autobiographical account was meant to suggest that Christianity was never quite able to penetrate this hinterland. The book became a best-seller and has been widely translated. It is still the best place for the outsider to gain an insight into the mentality of peasants in the Mezzogiorno of that era. A film, "Eboli," directed by Francesco Rosi, was made from the book in 1980. The classic overall treatment of the Southern Question is Friedrich Vöchting, *Die Italienische Südfrage* (Berlin, 1951), also available in Italian translation. Edward C. Banfield's sociological study of Lucania, *The Moral Basis of a Backward Society* (Glencoe, Ill., 1958), raises doubts as to the likelihood of rapid change. Nevertheless, history has a way of moving forward in spite of scholarly predictions. Important changes have occurred in the South—as is quickly apparent to a returning visitor who goes there in 1980 and contrasts it with the situation at war's end. Margaret Carlyle, a British specialist, has written a brief account, *The Awakening of Southern Italy* (New York, 1962), which can be supplemented by Leonard W. Moss's chapter, "The Passing of Traditional Peasant Society in the South," pp. 147-70 in *Modern Italy: A Topical History Since 1861*, ed. Edward R. Tannenbaum and Emiliana P. Noether, already cited.

A study, *Fate and Honor, Family and Village: Demographic and Cultural*

Change in Rural Italy since 1800 (Chicago, 1980), by Rudolph M. Bell, an ethnohistorian, describes four country villages in southern and central Italy. He rejects the stereotype of the peasantry as tragic, backward, hopeless, downtrodden, static, and passive. Instead, he contends that they are active, flexible, and shrewd, participating fully in shaping their destinies. Bell suggests four concepts that he feels capture the essence of the Italian peasant's life: *fortuna* (fate), *onore* (honor, dignity), *famiglia* (family), and *campanilismo* (village). Feliks Gross's *Il Paese: Values and Social Change in an Italian Village* (New York, 1973) is a comparative study of the changes that have taken place between 1957 and 1971 in Bonagente, a town in Frosinone province. Gross expresses concern that rapid innovation and modernization may destroy paramount esthetic values and traditions of the village culture. Central Italy has also attracted the attention of social anthropologists. Sydel Silverman's monograph, *Three Bells of Civilization: The Life of an Italian Hill Town* (New York, 1975), analyzes the "civilization" of the Umbrian town of Montecastello di Vibio, which overlooks the Tiber valley. *Patrons and Partisans: A Study of Politics in Two Southern Italian Comuni* (London, 1980), by Caroline White, challenges some of the stereotypes about southern politics. Her comparative examination of the complexities of political relations in two villages in the Fucino basin of the Abruzzi reveals that one village was organized on the basis of patron-clientelism, whereas the other encouraged participation in the political parties and voluntary associations. This is the same area whose difficult life during the Fascist dictatorship was poignantly described by the political exile, Ignazio Silone, in his novels, *Fontamara* (New York, 1934) and *Bread and Wine* (New York, 1937; rev. ed., 1962).

Ann Cornelisen's recent book, *Flight from Torregreca* (London, 1980), describes with sympathy the problems facing emigrants from an anonymous southern village when they move into the labor markets of the North and of Germany. Of interest, too, is Joseph Lopreato, *Peasants No More: Social Change in an Underdeveloped Society* (San Francisco, 1967), a study of Calabria.

Italy's rate of population growth has been declining sharply in recent decades. Already some sections in the North have achieved "zero population growth," while the entire nation should reach this condition by the 1990s. Between 1974 and 1979 the nation's population grew from about 55,385,000 to 56,877,000—a 2.7% increase.

Part of this growth was attributable to "guest-workers" who have been flocking into Italy from North Africa and elsewhere. Robert E. Dickinson's *The Population Problem of Southern Italy: An Essay in Social Geography* (Syracuse, 1955), although dated, was a straightforward presentation of the data then available. A demographic study that is not confined just to the South is Massimo Livi-Bacci, *A History of Italian Fertility during the Last Two Centuries* (Princeton, 1977).

There are a number of studies of the Mafia. Norman Lewis, *The Honoured Society, the Mafia Conspiracy Observed* (London, 1964), deals with the period since 1943. He presents a vivid and depressing picture of the economic bondage of western Sicily, which at the end of World War II remained little different from what it was like in Garibaldi's day. Michele Pantaleone, *The Mafia and Politics* (New York, 1966), is the work of a courageous Italian observer. For a backward look at the Mafia during Mussolini's dictatorship and at the moment of liberation, one can turn to Jack E. Reece, "Fascism, the Mafia, and the Emergence of Sicilian Separatism (1919–1943)," *Journal of Modern History* 45 (June 1973): 261–76. Covering a longer period and dealing with a particular village is Anton Blok, *The Mafia of a Sicilian Village, 1860–1960: A Study of Violent Peasant Entrepreneurs* (New York, 1975).

Sidney G. Tarrow, *Peasant Communism in Southern Italy* (New Haven, 1967), is an excellent study of the problems facing the Communist party in a region where classes are amorphous and shifting, and where there has been no tradition among the masses of looking to a political party for salvation. *Report from Palermo* (New York, 1959), by Danilo Dolci, a Sicilian reformer, combines moral fervor with some shrewd social analysis.

Cultural Life in the Twentieth Century

The best starting place in English in this field is H. Stuart Hughes's richly textured *Consciousness and Society: The Orientation of European Social Thought, 1890–1930,* mentioned before. Hughes treats a number of prominent Italians, including Croce, Pareto, Mosca, and Gramsci. His book can be supplemented by James H. Meisel, *The Myth of the Ruling Class: Gaetano Mosca and the "Elite"* (Ann Arbor, 1958), and in Italian by Ettore A. Albertini, *Gaetano Mosca: Storia di una dottrina politica. Formazione e interpretazione* (Milan, 1978). Robert Wohl, *The Generation of 1914* (Cambridge,

Mass., 1979), is an innovative study of mentalities and generational consciousness. It includes a chapter on Italy in which he examines the outlook of a cross section of young intellectuals on the eve of the Great War.

Numerous studies of the influential Neapolitan philosopher and historian Benedetto Croce (1866-1954) have appeared. A sympathetic early one, *Benedetto Croce* (New Haven, 1952), was written by Cecil J. S. Sprigge, a British journalist well acquainted with Italy. The shrewdest assessment of Croce's historical scholarship is the essay by Federico Chabod, "Croce storico," *Rivista storica italiana* 64 (1952): 473-530. Denis Mack Smith has presented a rather hostile judgment of Croce's conservative politics and his initially tolerant view of Fascism in "Historians in Politics: Benedetto Croce," *Journal of Contemporary History* 8 (Jan. 1973): 41-62. Croce completely reversed his attitude toward Fascism after 1925, it should be kept in mind. Thus there is no reason to doubt that his subsequent, "quiet" anti-Fascism gave much moral encouragement to intellectuals during the dictatorship. Sandro Setta's study of the 1943-52 period, *Croce, il liberalismo e l'Italia postfascista* (Bari, 1979), suffers from an often hostile Marxist bias against Croce. Angelo A. de Gennaro has written a small book that touches on the panoply of Croce's intellectual interests, *The Philosophy of Benedetto Croce* (New York, 1961), while in Italian there is Michele Abbate, *La filosofia di Benedetto Croce e la crisi della società italiana* (Turin, 1966). A selection of translated "essays on the moral and political problems of our time" may be found in Croce's *My Philosophy* (New York, 1949; reprint, 1962), ed. Raymond Klibansky. The major biography is *Benedetto Croce* (Turin, 1962), written by Fausto Nicolini, a close friend of Croce. The journal, *Rivista di studi crociani,* is published in Naples at Croce's Istituto italiano per gli studi storici.

Henry S. Harris has written on Giovanni Gentile (1875-1944), the Sicilian idealist philosopher of "actualism" who severed his once close ties with Croce and offered enthusiastic support to Fascism for the rest of his life and served for a time as its minister of education in the 1920s: *The Social Philosophy of Giovanni Gentile* (Urbana, Ill., 1960).

Among the cogent examinations of the ways in which Italian intellectuals responded to Fascism are the essay by Emiliana P. Noether, "Italian Intellectuals under Fascism," *Journal of Modern*

History 43 (Dec. 1971): 630-48, and the chapter by Paolo Vita-Finzi, "Italian Fascism and the Intellectuals," in *The Nature of Fascism*, ed. Stuart J. Woolf (New York, 1968). H. Stuart Hughes's chapter, "The Critique of Fascism," in *The Sea Change: The Migration of Social Thought, 1930-1965* (New York, 1975)—the last volume of his trilogy surveying European social thought since 1890—discusses the writings on this subject by such émigrés in America as Gaetano Salvemini and Giuseppe A. Borgese. Another anti-Fascist intellectual who was driven out of Italy to France, where he died in 1926, was Piero Gobetti, the influential young editor of Turin's *Rivoluzione liberale*. His philosophy was to exert some influence on both Carlo Rosselli's clandestine Giustizia e Libertà movement and the Action party of the Resistance era. Gobetti's collected works, "Opere complete," 3 vols. (Turin, 1969-74), have been edited by Paolo Spriano. Umberto Morra is preparing a biography for the Valeri series. References to a number of anti-Fascist émigrés may also be found in *Illustrious Immigrants: The Intellectual Migration from Europe, 1930-41* (Chicago, 1968), by Laura Fermi, widow of the Italian nuclear physicist, Enrico Fermi, who came to the University of Chicago in 1938 and received a Nobel Prize the following year. She has written *Atoms in the Family: My Life with Enrico Fermi* (Chicago, 1954). Aldo Garosci's book, *Gli intellettuali e la guerra di Spagna* (Turin, 1959), is full of fascinating observations about the reactions of intellectuals from a number of countries to the Spanish Civil War—a conflict in which Garosci fought alongside Rosselli's Giustizia e Libertà volunteers in defense of Catalan republicanism. Finally, Tannenbaum's *The Fascist Experience: Italian Society and Culture, 1922-1945,* cited earlier, contains some good chapters.

In the field of literature, mention should be made of Sergio Jerry Pacifici, *A Guide to Contemporary Italian Literature: From Futurism to Neorealism* (Cleveland, 1962), and his *The Modern Italian Novel*, 3 vols. (Carbondale, 1967-79), as well as of Giuliano Manacorda, *Letteratura e cultura del periodo fascista* (Milan, 1974), and *Storia della letteratura italiana contemporanea, 1940-1975* (4th ed., Rome, 1977). Two important studies of the Sicilian dramatist Luigi Pirandello are Walter Starkie, *Luigi Pirandello, 1867-1936* (3rd rev. ed., Berkeley, 1965), and Gaspare Giudice, *Pirandello: A Biography* (London, 1975).

On the Italian cinema, which has enjoyed worldwide acclaim, there are informative studies by Vernon Jarratt, *The Italian Cinema*

(New York, 1952), and Pierre Leprohon, *The Italian Cinema* (New York, 1972). The latter examines the major films in the framework of postwar political and social crises. Gianni Rodolino's *Storia del cinema* (Turin, 1977) will be complemented by a biography of the director, Luchino Visconti, for the Valeri series.

Ada Louise Huxtable's biography, *Pier Luigi Nervi* (New York, 1960), is a good study of the renowned architect (b. 1891; d. 1979) who designed out of reinforced concrete the sports palace in Rome's modern EUR district for the 1960 Olympic Games. Studies by Agnoldomenico Pica, *Cento anni di edilizia* (Rome, 1963) and *Pier Luigi Nervi* (Rome, 1969), are also important.

The Futurist movement of Filippo Marinetti (1876-1944) influenced politics, art, and literature. James Joll is chiefly concerned with politics in his essay on Marinetti in *Intellectuals in Politics* (London, 1960). Marianne W. Martin, *Futurist Art and Theory, 1909-1915* (Oxford, 1968), and Rosa T. Clough, *Futurism: The Story of a Modern Art Movement: A New Appraisal* (New York, 1961), are good on art.

Postwar Foreign Policy

Though relatively restricted, the literature on this theme is growing. Norman Kogan has offered insights into the role of pressure groups and political ideologies in his analytical study, *The Politics of Italian Foreign Policy* (New York, 1963). It clarifies the constraints that undergird Italian foreign policy.

We have a number of memoirs by Italian diplomats, including Alberto Tarchiani, who was ambassador to the United States during the first decade after the war: *Dieci anni tra Roma e Washington* (Milan, 1955), and those of Foreign Minister Carlo Sforza, *Cinque anni a Palazzo Chigi: La politica estera italiana dal 1947 al 1951* (Rome, 1952). Livio Zeno's profile, *Ritratto di Carlo Sforza* (Florence, 1976), points out this statesman's vigorous support of European integration. Raffaele Guariglia's *Ricordi, 1922-1946* (Naples, 1949), are informative on the diplomacy of the Fascist era and of the ensuing Badoglio government in which he served as foreign minister.

There is a good chapter on the Paris peace settlement of 1947 in *The Semblance of Peace: The Political Settlement After the Second World War* (New York, 1972), by John W. Wheeler-Bennett and Anthony Nicholls. John C. Cámpbell, ed., *Successful Negotiation: Trieste, 1954, An Appraisal by the Five Participants* (Princeton, 1976), clarifies the complex diplomatic moves surrounding this postwar dispute. Mario Toscano, who was the official historian of the Ministry of Foreign Affairs, has compiled a pro-Italian account of the negotiations with Austria over *Alto Adige and South Tyrol: Italy's Frontier with the German World*, ed. George A. Carbone (Baltimore, 1976). Anthony Evelyn Alcock, *The History of the South Tyrol Question* (London and Geneva, 1970), tends to be more objective. A number of essays by Italians on a variety of topics are to be found in Massimo Bonanni, ed., *La politica estera della Repubblica italiana*, 3 vols. (Milan, 1967).

Probably the most important book on postwar foreign policy is F. Roy Willis, *Italy Chooses Europe* (New York, 1971). The author is well informed about the postwar movement for European integration and Italy's role in it. Italy's underlying strategy has been to try to solve its internal political and economic problems by shifting them from a national to an international context whenever possible. Some modest success has already been achieved in gaining financial assistance from the EEC's Regional Development Fund for Italy's underdeveloped South. Primo Vannicelli's study, *Italy, NATO, and the European Community: The Interplay of Foreign Policy and Domestic Politics* (Cambridge, Mass., 1974), provides further evidence of Italy's strategy. The Italian Communist party has now come to accept the country's membership in both the EEC and NATO, but with certain reservations regarding the latter.

The energy crisis since 1973 has pointed up Italy's heavy dependence on imported oil and gas. Much of Italy's oil comes from Libya, whose *nouveaux riches* have recently been investing some of their profits in Fiat. Fiat, incidentally, has provided much engineering expertise for Soviet Russia's new automobile manufacturing center, Tolyatti. Italy's changing posture in the international economy is also shown by the fact that now she faces a social problem of "guest-workers," most of whom hail from North Africa.

All of these considerations help to condition Italy's foreign policy. It seems safe to say, however, that a generation after the overthrow of the Fascist dictatorship, Italy remains securely anchored in the European Community and the North Atlantic Treaty Organization and is one of the most vigorous advocates of strengthening the powers of the popularly elected European Parliament. Italy's present-day Europeanism thus marks a significant and welcome shift away from the predominantly nationalistic outlook of *sacro egoismo* that characterized much of her leadership at the start of this century.

Index of Authors

Abbate, Michele 72
Adams, John Clarke 61
Agarossi, Elena 55
Alatri, Paolo 20-21, 48
Albertini, Ettore A. 71
Albertini, Luigi 15, 18
Albrecht-Carrié, René 19
Albright, David E. 64
Alcock, Anthony E. 75
Allardyce, Gilbert 43
Allen, Kevin 68
Allum, P. A. 62
Andreotti, Giulio 58, 58fn, 67
Apih, Elio 32
Aquarone, Alberto 8fn, 11-12, 33-34, 35
Arfè, Gaetano 14, 28fn, 48
Asante, Samuel K. B. 45
Askew, William C. 17

Badoglio, Pietro 49
Baer, George W. 45
Banfield, Edward C. 69
Bariè, Ottavio 15
Barile, Paolo 61
Barker, A. J. 45
Barnes, Samuel H. 62
Barros, James 44
Battaglia, Roberto 55
Bell, Rudolph M. 69-70
Berengo, Marino 8
Bernardini, Gene 40
Berner, Wolfgang 64
Berselli, Aldo 35
Bertoldi, Silvio 13, 49, 50
Bianchi, Gianfranco 48-49, 55
Binchy, Daniel A. 37
Blackmer, Donald L. M. 64
Blok, Anton 71
Blumenson, Martin 50, 51
Bocca, Giorgio 47, 50, 55, 63, 66
Bonanni, Massimo 75
Bonomi, Ivanoe 51, 52fn
Bosworth, Richard J. 8, 16
Bottai, Giuseppe 36
Briani, Vittorio 18
Brown, Benjamin F. 20
Bucci, P. Vincent 68
Bütler, Hugo 28fn
Butler, James R. M. 51
Byé, Maurice 69

Cadorna, Raffaele 54
Caizzi, Bruno 35
Cammett, John H. 63

Campbell, John C. 74-75
Candeloro, Giorgio 12, 19
Cannistraro, Philip V. 6fn, 24, 36, 37, 45
Cantagalli, Roberto 32
Carbone, George A. 75
Cardoza, Anthony L. 32
Carli-Ballola, Renato 54
Carlyle, Margaret 69
Carocci, Giampiero 44
Carrillo, Eliza 38
Carsten, F. L. 43
Casanova, Antonio G. 47fn
Case, Lynn M. 8fn
Cassels, Alan 8, 23, 42, 44
Castronovo, Valerio 14, 35
Catalano, Franco 12
Cervi, Mario 47
Ceva, Lucio 47
Chabod, Federico 16, 23, 29, 72
Ciano, Galeazzo 44
Cipolla, Carlo M. 68
Clark, Martin 63
Clough, Rosa T. 74
Clough, Shepard B. 68
Coffey, Thomas M. 45
Cohen, Jon S. 17
Colapietra, Raffaele 58
Colarizi, Simona 32
Coles, Harry L. 52
Collier, Richard 24
Coppa, Frank J. 14, 24
Cordasco, Francesco 18
Cordova, Ferdinando 27-28, 44
Cornelisen, Ann 70
Corner, Paul 31
Coverdale, John F. 46
Cox, Geoffrey 56
Craig, Gordon A. 44
Cremona, Paul 43
Cresciani, Gianfranco 8
Croce, Benedetto 13, 14, 40, 52, 72

Davis, John A. 63
Davis, Melton S. 49
Deakin, F. William 24, 49
De Caprariis, Vittorio 19fn
De Caro, Gaspare 28fn
Decleva, Enrico 58
De Felice, Renzo 8, 9, 12, 20. 25-27, 30, 39-40
De Gasperi, Alcide 38, 58
De Gasperi, Maria Romana Catti '57fn-58fn
De Grand, Alexander J. 31, 36

77

Delzell, Charles 6fn, 9, 22fn, 23, 23fn, 24fn, 39, 42, 47-48, 54, 55fn
Demers, Francis J. 32
De Risio, Carlo 47
De Rosa, Gabriele, 15; 38
Dickinson, Robert E. 71
Diggins, John P. 34-35
Di Nolfo, Ennio 10, 44
Di Palma, Giuseppe 61
Di Scala, Spencer 14
Dolci, Danilo 71
Domenach, J. M. 64
Dorso, Guido 26
Dugan, James 45

Earle, Edward Meade 30fn
Earle, John 61
Ehrman, John 51
Einaudi, Luigi 9, 19, 58
Einaudi, Mario 58, 64, 69
Ellwood, David W. 52, 55
Evans, Robert H. 62, 64

Falconi, Carlo 67
Faldella, Emilio 47
Fermi, Laura 24, 73
Ferrarotti, Franco 64
Finer, Herman 32-33
Fiori, Giuseppe 63
Fisher, Ernest F., Jr. 51
Fonzi, Fausto 15
Fornari, Harry 32
Fortunato, Giustino 40
Francovich, Carlo 48
Frankel, P. H. 69
Frassati, Luciana 14-15
Fried, Robert C. 61, 62

Gaeta, Franco 31
Galli, Giorgio 59, 62, 64
Gallo, Max 24-25
Gambino, Antonio 58
Gardner, Albert N. 50
Garosci, Aldo 6, 48, 64, 73
Gennaro, Angelo A. de 72
Gentile, Emilio 31
Germani, Gino 34
Germino, Dante L. 35, 61
Gilbert, Felix 44
Giolitti, Giovanni 13
Giudice, Gaspare 27, 73
Gobetti, Piero 40, 73
Gorresio, Vittorio 64
Gramsci, Antonio 9, 63
Gregor, A. James 30, 34, 42
Grew, Raymond 11

Griffith, William E. 64
Grindrod, Muriel 11, 58
Gross, Feliks 70
Guariglia, Raffaele 74
Guerri, Giordano Bruno 44

Halperin, S. William 23
Hamilton, Alastair 34
Harris, Charles R. S. 52
Harris, Henry S. 72
Hess, Robert L. 18
Hibbert, Christopher 24
Hildebrand, George H. 69
Hoepke, K.-P. 46
Holland, Stuart 68
Horowitz, Daniel L. 68
Howard, Michael 51
Hughes, H. Stuart 11, 23, 30fn, 44, 58-59, 71
Humphrey, Richard 30fn
Huxtable, Ada Louise 74

Iggers, Georg G. 8
Ilardi, Vincent 8fn

Jackson, William G. F. 51
Jarratt, Vernon 73-74
Jemolo, Arturo Carlo 37
Joll, James 63, 74
Jullian, Philippe 20

Kaplan, Morton A. 64
Katz, Robert 39, 49, 67
Kelikian, A. A. 32
Kertzer, David I. 64
Kirkpatrick, Ivone 24
Knox, MacGregor 47
Kogan, Norman 52, 59-60, 61, 65, 74
Koon, Tracy H. 36
Kurzman, Dan 51

Lafore, Laurence 45
Landuyt, Ariane 47fn
Lange, Peter 61
La Palombara, Joseph 61, 68, 69
Laqueur, Walter 42, 65, 66-67
Larsen, Stein Ugelvik 43
Lavine, Marcia F. 44
Ledeen, Michael A. 20, 26, 26fn, 36, 44
Lederer, Ivo 20
Leonhard, Wolfgang 65
Leprohon, Pierre 74
Levi, Carlo 69
Levi, Fabio 9
Levra, Umberto 9
Lewanski, R. J. and R. C. 8fn

Lewis, Norman 55, 71
Linz, Juan J. 42
Livi-Bacci, Massimo 71
Longo, Luigi 54
Lopreato, Joseph 70
Lowe, Cedric J. 43
Lutz, Vera 69
Lytle, Scott H. 30fn
Lyttelton, Adrian 29, 31, 43

MacGregor-Hastie, Roy 24
Macartney, Maxwell H. H. 43
Mack Smith, Denis 10, 11, 46, 72
McInnes, Neil 64
Macmillan, Harold 52
Maier, Charles S. 34, 43
Mammarella, Giuseppe 58, 62
Manacorda, Giuliano 73
Margiotta Broglio, Francesco 37
Martin, Marianne W. 74
Marzari, F. 43
Megaro, Gaudens 29-30
Meisel, James H. 30fn, 71
Melograni, Pietro 19, 35
Mercuri, Lamberto 52
Michaelis, Meir 39
Middlemas, Keith 65
Miller, James E. 55
Mira, Giovanni 6, 22-23
Molony, John N. 38
Monelli, Paolo 24
Monticone, Alberto 19
Morley, John F. 39
Morra, Umberto 73
Moss, Leonard W. 69
Mussolini, Benito 20, 21, 30-31, 49

Nenni, Pietro 60-61
Neufeld, Maurice F. 68
Nicholls, Anthony 74
Nicolini, Fausto 72
Nigro, Louis J. 19
Noether, Emiliana P. 6fn, 10, 11, 20, 69, 72-73
Nolte, Ernst 40fn, 40-41

Omodeo, Adolfo 23
O. S. S. 55
Ostenc, Michel 36

Pacifici, Sergio J. 73
Palla, Marco 32
Pantaleone, Michele 71
Parker, Harold T. 8
Parri, Ferruccio 56fn
Passigli, Stefano 61

Paulson, Belden 64
Pavone, Claudio 8-9
Payne, Stanley G. 42
Peck, George T. 23fn
Perfetti, Francesco 31
Perticone, Giacomo 12
Petersen, Jens 35, 46
Pica, Agnoldomenico 74
Pieroni Bortolotti, Franca 37
Pieri, Piero 19, 49
Pini, Giorgio 25
Piscitelli, Enzo 58
Poggi, Gianfranco 62
Posner, M. V. 68
Poulantzas, Nikos 43
Poulat, Émile 15
Prandi, Alfonso 62
Preti, Luigi 36, 40
Procacci, Giuliano 11
Puntoni, Paolo 49

Quazza, Guido 35-36, 55

Ragionieri, Ernesto 55
Rainero, Romain 18
Ranney, Austin 65
Reece, Jack E. 71
Rhodes, Anthony 20, 39
Ricci, Athos 64
Riscossa, Sergio 68
Roberts, David D. 30
Robertson, Esmonde M. 45
Rochat, Giorgio 17fn, 19, 45, 49
Rodolino, Gianni 74
Rodotà, Stefano 8fn
Rogari, Sandro 37
Rogger, Hans 43
Romano, Ruggiero 12
Romano, Salvatore F. 12, 63
Romano, Sergio 17fn
Romeo, Rosario 10, 11, 63
Rosengarten, Frank 48
Rosenstock-Franck, Louis 33
Rosoli, Gianfausto 37
Rossi, Ernesto 35, 69
Rossini, Giovanni 47fn
Roth, Jack J. 30, 30fn
Roveri, Alessandro 32
Rumi, Giorgio 44
Rusinow, Dennison I. 45

Sacco, Giuseppe 64
Saladino, Salvatore 14
Salomone, A. William 8, 13-14, 23fn
Salvadori, Massimo 11, 54
Salvatorelli, Luigi 6, 22-23, 23fn, 26

79

Salvemini, Gaetano 6, 14, 23fn, 28, 33, 44, 45
Sani, Giacomo 64
Santarelli, Enzo 23
Sarti, Roland 33
Sartori, Giovanni 65
Schmidt, Carl T. 33
Schmitt, Hans 23
Schröder, Josef 47
Scoppola, Pietro 15, 58fn
Sechi, Salvatore 32
Segrè, Claudio 17, 17fn
Seton-Watson, Christopher 10, 16, 18, 43
Setta, Sandro 57, 72
Sforza, Carlo 74
Shay, Mary L. 8fn
Siebert, Ferdinand 47
Silj, Alessandro 66
Silone, Ignazio 70
Silverman, Sydel 70
Silvestri, Stefano 64
Sirugo, Francesco 27
Smith, Bradley F. 55
Smyth, Howard McGaw 50, 56
Sonnino, Sidney 20
Sorel, Georges 30
Sori, Ercole 18
Spadolini, Giovanni 15
Spini, Giorgio 60
Spriano, Paolo 48, 58, 62
Sprigge, Cecil J. S. 72
Squeri, Laurence L. 32
Starkie, Walter 73
Stevenson, Andrew 68
Sturzo, Luigi 9, 38
Susmel, Duilio 25, 30fn, 44

Talamo, Giuseppe 15
Tamaro, Attilio 23
Tamburrano, Giuseppe 60–61
Tannahill, R. Neal 64
Tannenbaum, Edward R. 11, 23fn, 36, 69, 73
Tarchiani, Alberto 74
Tarrow, Sidney 61, 62, 64, 71
Tasca, Angelo 28
Thayer, John A. 14
Thomas, D. H. 8fn
Togliatti, Palmiro 63
Tökés, Rudolf L. 65
Toscano, Mario 46, 49, 75
Tranfaglia, Nicola 9, 35
Traniello, Francesco 67fn

Ungari, Paolo 8fn, 31
Urban, George R. 26fn, 65

Viani, Mario 32
Valeri, Nino 12, 13, 19, 20, 21, 27, 28, 60, 68fn, 74
Valiani, Leo 13, 19fn, 48, 54, 55, 58
Vannicelli, Primo 75
Vaussard, Maurice 11
Vigezzi, Brunello 14, 16
Vita-Finzi, Paolo 73
Vivanti, Corrado 12
Vivarelli, Roberto 28–29, 48
Vöchting, Friedrich 69
Volpe, Gioacchino 13fn, 20
Votaw, Dow 69

Watt, D. C. 46
Webb, Leicester C. 68
Weber, Eugen 40, 43
Webster, Richard A. 16–17, 38
Weinberg, Albert K. 52
Welk, William G. 33
Wheeler-Bennett, John W. 74
White, Caroline 70
Whittam, John 18
Willis, F. Roy 75
Wiskemann, Elizabeth 23, 24, 46
Wohl, Robert 71–72
Woodward, Sir Llewellyn 50
Woolf, Stuart J. 10fn, 28, 43, 58, 68, 73

Zangrandi, Ruggero 36, 49
Zeno, Livio 74

80